CORNISH WALKS

WALKING IN THE MEVAGISSEY AREA

LIZ HURLEY

MUDLARK'S PRESS

First Edition, 2017

ISBN: 9780993218033

A CIP catalogue record for this book is available from the British Library

Typeset in PT Sans and PT Serif by Annabel Brandon

Mudlark's Press
www.hurleybooks.co.uk

CONTENTS

INTRODUCTION

Welcome to *Cornish Walks*. This series is designed to help you explore an area in greater depth and will feature a wide range of walks.

Each walk is circular so you can walk in either direction, although the guide only explains the route one way. If you want a longer walk, just retrace your footsteps for a change of scenery.

If you do all the walks and their extensions in this book, you will have walked almost 40 miles. You will have travelled from the Iron Age to the Industrial Revolution and beyond. You will have stood in the place of lost gardens and hidden wonders and hopefully also spotted some Cornish wildlife as well.

As these are largely countryside / coastal walks, the majority will not be suitable for wheelchairs or buggies.

The Mevagissey trail is the most adaptable for all wheels.

The National Cycle Trail 3 is also good for wheels. Some of the walks share part of the trail, and these sections would also be suitable, although not the whole walk. These are Walks 2, 3 & 5. Walk 6 may be suitable for cross-terrain buggies.

I have also taken into account walking with dogs. I walk with two Spaniels myself and find them the most challenging of dogs, and I use them as my benchmark. When I say challenging, I mean that they enjoy being off the lead and roaming. So I tend not to take them on walks where there is traffic or a lot of livestock. For the same reason, I like car parks that end near water.

Walk 5 is brilliant for dogs.

Throughout the guide are snippets of information regarding the landscape around you and always a recommendation for a good place to eat. Each walk also features links to further information and a link to a photo gallery of sights from the walk.

INSTRUCTIONS

COUNTRY CODE

- Respect the people who live and work in the countryside. Respect private property, farmland and all rural environments.
- Do not interfere with livestock, machinery and crops.
- Respect and, where possible protect all wildlife, plants and trees.
- When walking, use the approved routes and keep as closely as possible to them.
- Take special care when walking on country roads.
- Leave all gates as you find them and do not interfere with or damage any gates, fences, walls or hedges.
- Guard against all risks of fire, especially near forests.
- Always keep children closely supervised while on a walk.
- Do not walk the Ways in large groups and always maintain a low profile.
- Take all litter home - leaving only footprints behind.
- Keep the number of cars used to the minimum and park carefully to avoid blocking farm gateways or narrow roads.
- Minimise impact on fragile vegetation and soft ground.

Take heed of warning signs - they are there for your protection.

Dogs - The Countryside Code states that:

- By law, you must keep your dog under effective control so that it does not disturb or scare farm animals or wildlife. On most areas of open country and common land, known as 'access land' you must keep your dog on a short lead on most areas of open country and common land between 1 March and 31 July, and all year round near farm animals.
- You do not have to put your dog on a lead on public paths, as long as it is under close control. But as a general rule, keep your dog on a lead if you cannot rely on its obedience. By law, farmers are entitled to destroy a dog that injures or worries their animals.
- If livestock chase you and your dog, it is safer to let your dog off the lead – don't risk getting hurt by trying to protect it.
- Take particular care that your dog doesn't scare sheep and lambs or wander where it might disturb birds that nest on the ground and other wildlife – eggs and young will soon die without protection from their parents.
- Everyone knows how unpleasant dog mess is and it can cause infections – so always clean up after your dog and get rid of the mess responsibly. Also make sure your dog is wormed regularly to protect it, other animals and people.
- At certain times, dogs may not be allowed on some areas of access land or may need to be kept on a lead. Please follow any signs.

Cattle

If you find yourself in a field of suddenly wary cattle, move away as carefully and quietly as possible, and if you feel threatened by cattle then let go of your dog's lead and let it run free rather than try to protect it and endanger yourself. The dog will outrun the cows, and it will also outrun you.

Those without canine companions should follow similar advice: move away calmly, do not panic and make no sudden noises. Chances are the cows will leave you alone once they establish that you pose no threat.

If you walk through a field of cows and there happen to be calves, think twice; if you can, go another way and avoid crossing fields.

GUIDE TO THE LEGEND

Before heading off on a walk read the description first. You may discover issues with it. Cows, amount of stiles, mud etc. Then have a look at a map, not the little one provided with the walk to get a proper feel for the direction of the walk.

LENGTH: This has been calculated using a range of GPS tracking devices.
EFFORT: Easy to Strenuous. These descriptions are only in relation to each other in this book. Every walk has at least one hill in it, not everyone finds hills easy. Strenuous, this is for the hardest walks in the book, it will be based on effort and duration. However, nothing in here is particularly tortuous.
TERRAIN: If it's been raining a lot, please assume that footpaths will be muddy. Coast paths tend to be a bit better.
FOOTWEAR: I usually walk in walking boots, trainers or ridge sole wellingtons. Except for the two village walks, smart shoes, sandals, heels or flip flops are unsuitable.
SUITABLE FOR: A quick description of the walk. Due to the terrain of the walks, most are unsuitable for wheeled traffic. Only a few are suitable for wheelchairs and pushchairs.
COWS / SHEEP: It is possible that you won't encounter any livestock on a walk that mentions them. Please read the countryside code section, on how to avoid them if you do.
PARKING: Postcode for sat nav given.
TOILETS: Due to council cuts, lots of loos are now closed or run by local parishes with seasonal opening hours. If they will be an essential part of your walk check online first. Lots are now coin operated.
OS MAP: This will be the largest scale available for the area.
DIRECTIONS: If I say, "going up the road" up or down means there is a slope. If I refer to North or SW, you will need a compass. Most smartphones have built-in compasses. It won't be essential as other directions will be given, but it will be an aide. Especially in woodland where there are few other clues.

IN SIZE OF SCALE, LARGEST TO SMALLEST: Road, lane, unmade road, track, trail, path. Although some of the smaller descriptions are interchangeable.

OPTIONS: Several of the walks have options or alternate routes in order to avoid mud, cattle, seasonal access etc. You only need to choose one option but please read the whole section through first. It will help rule out any confusion.

1

MEVAGISSEY TRAIL

LENGTH: 2 miles
EFFORT: Easy, some steps, alternate routes available
TERRAIN: Road
FOOTWEAR: Any
SUITABLE FOR: Anyone, good for little feet. Buggies can avoid steps.
COWS / SHEEP/ HORSES: Mermaids and sea monsters
PARKING: Mevagissey
WCS: Mevagissey
CAFE / PUB: Various
OS MAP: 105

BRIEF DESCRIPTION: An enjoyable and detailed tour around this historic village

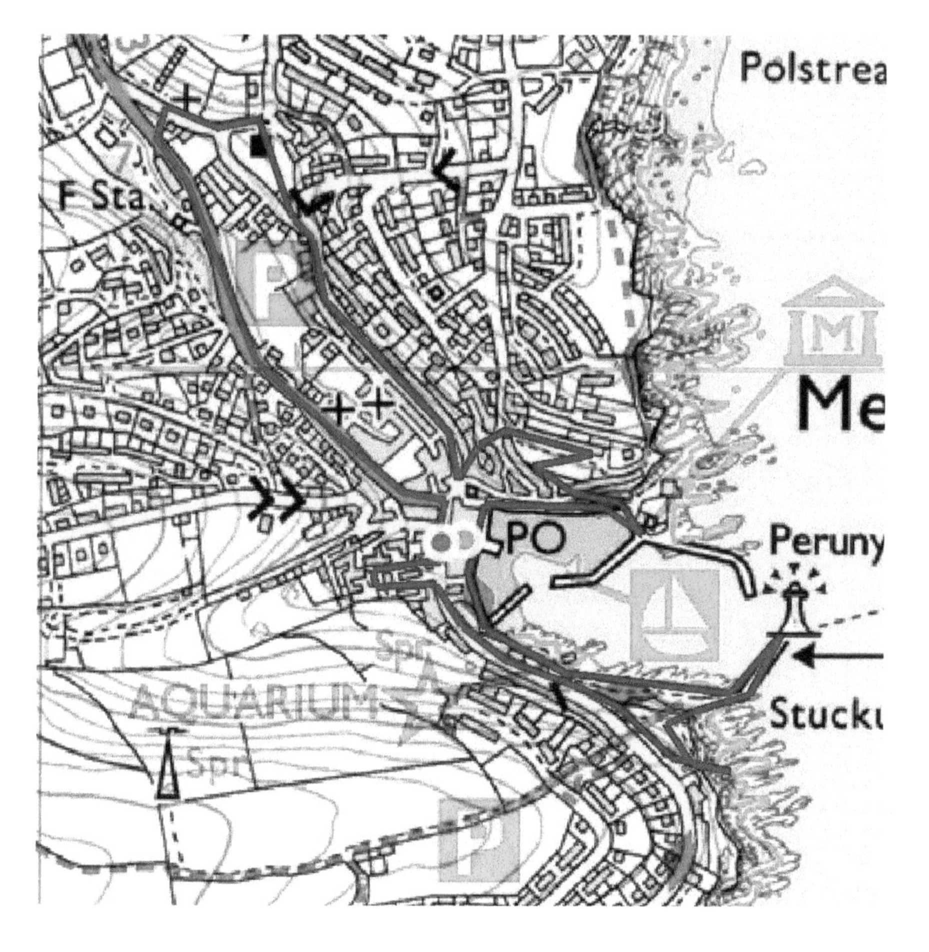

Elevation Profile

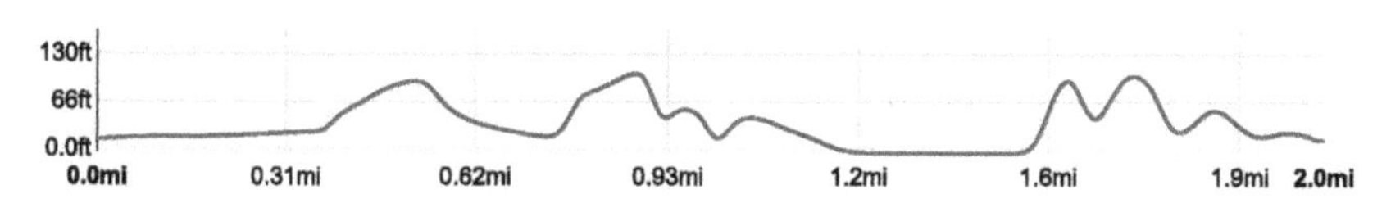

DIRECTIONS

1. From Hurley Books / Tourist Information Centre turn left up Jetty Street, away from the sea. Turn right onto Fore Street and then left at the Ship Inn. **See *The River Back* and *Waterwheel and Leat*.**

2. Now walk along Valley Road out of the village. Above and to your left is where the leat used to run, and to the right is the hidden river. The road you are on used to be a track and was only turned into the main St Austell road in the 1920s. As you pass the end of Willow Car Park, you will see a very large exit sign, just behind it is the river, if you fancy a quick peek. Walk past the sign and take the right-hand footpath through the lawn by the village sign. Go up the steps and when you join the road, turn right and head up towards the Church. When you get to the T-Junction turn left and head up around the edge of the church. Enter the churchyard through its footpath on your right. **See *Church* and *Cholera*.**

The River Back: This area is known as Town Bridge or Market Square or River Street. Given the topography of Mevagissey, sitting at the bottom of a steep valley beside the sea, it is not surprising that we should have a river but not many notice it, as for the most part it remains hidden, either underground or tucked behind buildings. The River Back skirts along the path leading towards Heligan and then alongside the park. It flows under the road by Willow Car Park. In the past, the river ran through this marshy field, populated with willows. The river can then be seen again running behind Chapel Street; Chapel Street used to be referred to as Back Lit.

The river's final appearance is through the grills on the road outside the leather shop where it finally flows into the harbour. For most of the year, the river flows underground and unnoticed until we get heavy rains when it makes its presence felt.

MEVAGISSEY HARBOUR

3. Leave the churchyard at the bottom and continue down Church Lane. Carry on back into the village as it joins Church Street. As Church Street opens into St George's Square, you will find yourself amongst shops and pubs. Turn left as you pass Brocante, towards the Fountain Inn. Immediately before the pub there is a tiny covered alleyway, called Shilly Alley Op, the name is up on the wall behind you.

4. Walk up behind the pub and follow the signs for "Bank Street leading to Bank Terrace" This is a winding flight of steps. You are now walking into the old area of Porthilly. At the top, turn right into "Bank Tce" at the T-junction turn left and then take the walkway directly on your right. This leads you onto Battery Terrace. **See *Battery Terrace*.**

5. Walk to the very end of Battery Terrace and talk the path on the right heading down, do not take any of the paths that lead into private gardens. The path now comes to an area of grass, and you can go left or right. If you go right through the unmade path in the grass, you will really get a sense of how riddled the pathways are. Follow the grass path, then turn left between a breeze block wall and a wooden fence, and follow the steps down as they wind through the cottages. Eventually, you will pop out in Cliff Street. There are no handrails or directions, and the surfaces are very uneven. (Continue p.12.)

Waterwheel and Leat: On old maps, we can see that the river was once split up by the football pitch and that a leat was created to power a waterwheel located where the RNLI and surrounding shops sit. This wheel powered the village flour mill. The leat and waterwheel have long since disappeared.

Church: This area was originally the second habitation of Mevagissey and was called Lammorek, Lammorek meaning Church by the Sea (morek meaning maritime, and lan/ lam being the old Cornish for Church.) It was first mentioned in Church records in 1259.

Cholera: In 1831 Mevagissey was struck down by a severe outbreak of cholera. A visual reminder of the numbers involved can be seen in the village graveyard. A tombstone for Peter Furse, who died from cholera, stands on its own. The land surrounding his stone was a mass pit for the dead who were too poor to mark their own burial site. In two months the village lost nearly 6% of its population. Despite this savage blow to the community, Mevagissey soon restored itself, primarily through the profits brought by the fishing industry.

If you look about you will see MM on some of the gravestones. MM stands for Master Mariner. This is the professional qualification required for someone to serve as the Captain of a commercial vessel of any size, of any type, operating anywhere in the world. The term has been in use at least since the 13th century, reflecting the fact that in guild or livery company terms, such a person was a Master in this specific profession.

Battery Terrace: Being a seaport, Mevagissey must have been continually involved in providing able seaman for the Navy, and many of our Master Mariners did their duty. According to Hitchens and Drew, writing in 1824, a battery of six, eighteen-pounder guns along the eastern edge of the village, was erected about the commencement of the American war in 1775. However, they were never called into use, nor were they during the following, Napoleonic conflict. Their location is now marked by the naming of "Battery Terrace", but other clues remain. If you look closely around Old Sands, near the Harbour Master's Office, you may notice some odd bollards where the boats tie up. These are what is left of the guns.

Running above and alongside Battery Terrace is the old Rope Walk, now a private garden and the Coastguard Cottages. Rope was made and laid out here for centuries, facing south and running flat it would have been a good location for drying and mending. The Coastguard Cottages are now also private residences.

Cliff Street Fishermen: Sculptor, Elinor Lambert made These little groups of fishermen found on some of the windowsills of Cliff Street in the 1950s. They are a fond tribute to the fishermen as they would lean over the cliff walls looking out over the harbour, putting the world to rights.

Porthilly: Porthilly was first mentioned in 1694 but certainly much older than that and probably the birthplace of Mevagissey itself. This was around the area we now know as East Wharf, Old Sands and Cliff Street. It is riddled with secret passage-ways, tiny alleyways, hidden cellars, concealed doorways and doorways in rooftops. Walk up around the little lanes and ops above the East Wharf, and you step back 300 years with each step you take.

Harbour: The earliest evidence we have for the harbour is around 1550 when a stone quay was built in the general location of the existing East Quay, jutting out from the Harbour Masters office towards West Quay. West Quay is on the other side of the harbour and houses the Ice House and Fish Stores. The beach and slipway in front of where you are

currently standing is known as Old Sand and is clearly where the fishing village began. The rocks behind, providing a level of protection that was then reinforced by the mediaeval harbour wall. This section of the harbour is known as Island Quay, and you can see in old paintings that these buildings were once accessed via a bridge. Across the harbour, the beach to the left of West Quay is known as Sandy Beach. Like all the beaches around the harbour, it is submerged at high tide.

Seventeen Seventy-Four marked the first meeting of the Mevagissey Harbour Trust and was held in the Ship Inn. The Harbour Trust is a charity that exists to protect and promote all users and uses of the harbour; tourists, sailors, traders and fishermen all have an equal footing. During this period, the eastern harbour wall was strengthened, and the West Quay (where the fish store now sits) was built along with the jetty and wharves running along the front of the harbour. East and West Quay enclosed the inner harbour. In a relatively short period, Mevagissey was recognised for the port that it had become and was viewed as an important location for coastal trade by Parliament. In 1895, Middle Wharf was built up to connect the jetty to West Wharf. Prior to this, the sea came right up to the buildings' walls. Reaching out beyond the Harbour Master's Office, North Pier was completed in 1897 and along with Victoria Pier, creating the outer harbour known as The Pool.

6. Alternatively turn left and walk towards the sea. Join the coast path and head back into the cottages. You will still get a sense of the age of the area. **See *Cliff Street Fisherman* and *Porthilly*.**

7. Walk down through the lanes on whatever path you choose until you are on East Wharf, walk alongside the harbour out to sea until you get to the Museum. You are now standing at the heart and birthplace of Mevagissey. **See *Harbour*** and ***Movie Sets*.**

8. Head back towards the village, as you get towards She Sells, there used to be a famous bench where all the village men would sit and put the world to rights. This was known as the Mevagissey Parliament. **See *Parliament*.**

9. Continue to walk around the harbour front, all these large buildings were once wharves connected to the port. Continue past the shops until you get to the public loos, this is the site of a tin mine. Later on, this was also the site of our first electric power station which powered the lighthouse and Fore Street making us one of the first places in the UK to have street lighting in 1895. Earlier street lamps had been run on pilchard oil. **See *Wheal Kendall*.**

10. Continue walking out along the harbour, until you get to the aquarium which was the site of the old lifeboat station. **See *Lifeboat*.**

Movie Sets: You may be forgiven for thinking that the holes that you can see along the top of East Quay are pilchard press holes. However, I have been reliably informed that these are the remnants of a movie set, *Next of Kin*, and were meant to be gun emplacements. Talking of guns, if you can see these holes you can probably also see the Napoleonic Gun being used as an upright bollard.

Parliament: "In front of our house (now She Sells) was a low bench seat where all the old, retired fishermen sat to smoke and chat, reminiscing about their seafaring days and pointing out where the young ones were going wrong. It was known as Mevagissey Parliament. The seat was continuous and went right across the small doorway into my Grandfather's workshop - one had to step over it to gain entry. My father bought a motorcycle and wanted to house it there, so grandfather (Claud Hunkin) made a flap in the seat. Unfortunately, the old men and the Harbour Trust objected and took him to court. Effie Hunkin was the clerk at the time, so it was Hunkin versus Hunkin! Judge Rawlings was obviously amused by the case as he said that he wasn't sure how the 'Parliament' was formed - whether by verbosity or force of arms, however, he ruled that whenever access was needed, Parliament must rise!" — Roly Deighton

Wheal Kendall: Whilst much of Cornwall is famed for its mining it's not something that springs to mind when you think about Mevagissey, but we did once have our very own mine right on the harbour. Wheal Kendall didn't last long though, and it's fair to say that there must have been more money in fishing.

Lifeboat: In 1869 a lifeboat station was built but only ran until 1930. It was prone to storm damage and eventually closed. During its short lifespan though it was home to three successive boats; the South Warwickshire, the John Arthur and the James Chisholm. In all, fifty-eight souls were saved during their sixty years of service. Before and after that, lifeboat cover was provided by Fowey. The lifeboat station now provides a home for the Mevagissey Aquarium, run by the Harbour Trust and funded by donations.

Great Storm: During a rare blizzard in 1891, this recently built pier was devastated with large chunks being completely washed away. To destroy a newly-constructed harbour either says a lot about the construction of the harbour or the ferocity of the storm. Indeed, this blizzard was a remarkable event. For five days the blizzard battered the south of England. Large areas of Cornwall were left under snowdrifts between eight and fifteen foot high. Villages were cut off for weeks, ships were thrown onto rocks, and much property was destroyed. It is estimated that 200 people died and 6000 livestock. In The Gazette, the UK's Official Public Record, the destruction of the Mevagissey pier and inability to man the lighthouse, was not announced until April 14th, almost a month later. Given the severity of the loss, it shows that it took a very long time to get the message to London. The country had come to a standstill. As Mevagissey is surrounded by steep hills, I imagine the villagers were cut off for days.

The pier was rebuilt, and by 1895 the lighthouse was one of the first in the country to be powered by electricity.

Methodism: You are now on the site of a large Wesleyan Chapel. One of John Wesley's early friendships in Mevagissey was with James Dunn. Dunn had seen the light and a few years later (1757) personally invited Wesley back to address the village and made his own premises available. As the years progressed Wesley regularly visited Mevagissey and Dunn hosted him until his congregation became too large,

11. Carry on out along the pier towards the lighthouse. **See *Great Storm*.**

12. Take the steps up at the edge of the cliff up onto Cliff Park. There is a path to the upper left that heads towards the large white block of flats. Go through the gate and out onto the Crow's Nest for a great view. Return to the field and take the path that leads to the left and onto Polkirt Hill. Head back down into the village admiring the large houses that would have belonged to the wealthy traders living away from the stink of the Cliff Street area.

13. As the road levels out, duck through the passageway on your left by the Kings Arms. **See *Methodism*.**

14. Walk on through the shared courtyard towards the World of Model Railways. In a very old wall to the left, you can see one of the few public remains of the pilchard industry. **See *Pilchard Press*.**

15. Now return back to Fore Street and then turn right into Jetty Street where you started.

and Dunn started to raise subscriptions for a meeting house. The Methodist faith grew in strength and numbers across the UK but nowhere was it more firmly embraced than in Cornwall.

Pilchard Press: To process the fish, they were first salted in brine tanks and then packaged in wooden casks. The casks had holes in the bottom, and a lid was placed on top to which weights were added in order to squeeze the oil from the fish. To further leverage the squeeze, a long pole was slotted into the hole in the wall, and weights were tied to the end of it. The pole rested on top of the lid and pressed the pilchard. The lids were then fitted, and the barrels were shipped out. Many buildings in the village were used for this process. Very few signs of these presses exist today; some are hidden behind protective walls, others are features in private homes. However, one set of press holes can still be viewed in an old wall in a private car park by the Model Railway Museum.

RETURNING HOME

LINKS:

http://www.mevagisseymuseum.com/
A History of Mevagissey by Liz Hurley

PHOTO ALBUM:

https://www.flickr.com/photos/97473606@N04/albums/72157686207884541

2

HELIGAN LOOP

LENGTH: 4.5 miles
EFFORT: One steep hill. Easy
TERRAIN: Woodland, cycle path. Often muddy.
FOOTWEAR: Walking Boots. In dry weather trainers etc. are fine.
SUITABLE FOR: A nice stroll and a great way to wander up to Heligan. Good for buggies, although there is a very steep section and mud may be an issue.
COWS / SHEEP/ HORSES: None.
PARKING: Mevagissey Long Stay Car parks. Willow Carpark / Sunny Corner. PL26 6RZ
WCS: Mevagissey
CAFE / PUB: Mevagissey
OS MAP: 105

BRIEF DESCRIPTION: This is an easy to follow short circular walk, following the perimeter of the famous Heligan Estate. Perfect to walk to from Mevagissey, rather than catch a bus.

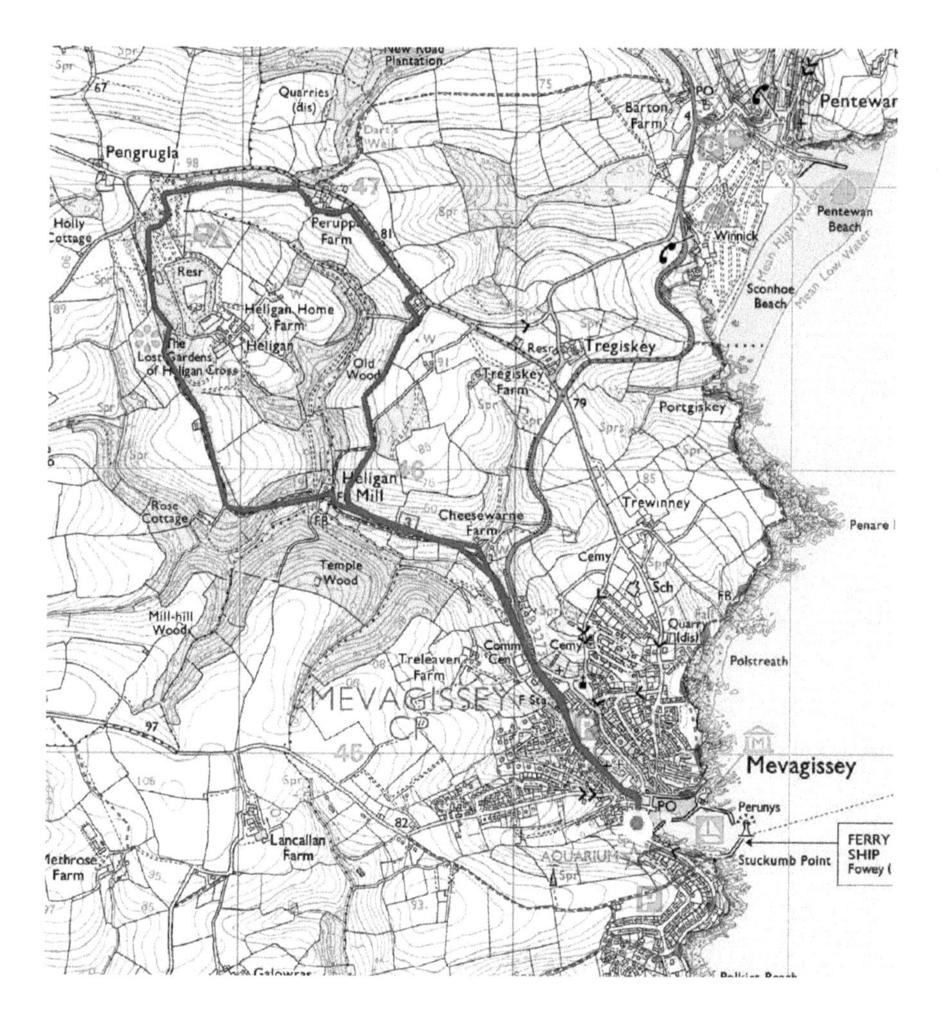

Elevation Profile

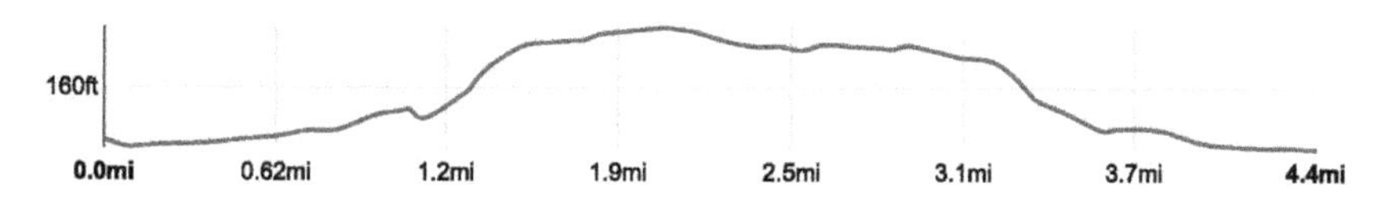

THE TRAIL AFTER HELIGAN MILL

FULL INSTRUCTIONS:

1. From your car park make your way onto the B3273, this is the main St Austell road leading out of the village. Head north in the St Austell direction. You will pass the bus stop and fire station on your left, as the road starts to head uphill, look to your left, by the Mevagissey Community Centre and you will see signs to Heligan going via the National Cycle Path, route 3. Take this path. Just as you reach your first mile, the path splits. **See *Heligan*.**

2. The cycle path veers towards the right, moving uphill, there is a path heading forward, staying on the flat, moving slightly to the left. This is your path and is usually labelled towards Heligan. During wet weather, this path can be very muddy. (Because this path is a loop if the footpath is too muddy, then just stay on the cycle trail instead). Follow this path to Heligan Mill, then cross over the small stream and continue through the

Heligan: The Heligan Estate was first recorded in the 1200s, it was taken over by the Tremayne family, with the house that we see today, being built in the 1700s. The Estate grew and prospered until the state of the First World War. Then the Estate workers along with many from the village enlisted and went off to war. The villages tended towards the Navy, but those from the Estate were land men and joined the army. The majority died, and the residing Tremayne owner moved to Italy, and the Estate fell into neglect. The house was split into flats in the seventies, but the gardens continued to be neglected until Tim Smit and John Wills, one of the Tremayne family, started to explore the grounds following the 1990 hurricane. They discovered the bones of a wonderful Victorian

cottages. Now head uphill on the unmade road. Follow this road all the way up to the top where it joins the Heligan Car park. **See *Heligan Mill.***

3. Cross the pelican crossing into the Heligan entrance area. Refreshments and loos are all before the ticket booth. To continue your walk, head out through the first car park (don't cross back over the pelican crossing) keep to the right-hand side of the car park, and three-quarters of the way down is a gate leading into the Heligan campsite. Go through here and into the site. Follow the site road left, to the campsite reception area. From here take the wide path on the right signposted Cycle Route 3 and Mevagissey. This path will lead all the way down and back into the village. Avoid any turning to Pentewan.

LINKS:

http://heligan.com/the-story/introduction/

PHOTO ALBUM:

https://www.flickr.com/photos/97473606@N04/albums/72157686207884531

Estate, with many of the features still standing, just. Over the next few decades, it has been restored and turned into the nations favourite garden, regularly voted by the nations favourite public garden.

The local or old way to pronounce Heligan is H'LIGG-un, emphasising the LIGG or just 'Ligun.

Heligan Mill: During the late 1940s, Mevagissey became a home for a variety of artists and writers. Often, they lived at Heligan Mill and were referred to by the village as a commune of bohemians. They spoke of communes and a better, more Utopian way of living. Not all in the circle were so optimistic and, sadly, attempted suicides, affairs and accidental deaths were the fate of some of them. Maybe they were just unhinged dreamers, as some of the local fishermen believed. Few left such an enduring mark as architect John Archibald Campbell. The three houses at the end of Chapel Point were designed by him, and they are breathtaking examples of art deco architecture and were meant to be the forerunners of a Utopian housing project that he had submitted plans for. Unfortunately, one evening he walked off a cliff and died.

3

MEVAGISSEY - PENTEWAN - PORTGISKY - MEVAGISSEY

LENGTH: 5 miles
EFFORT: Strenuous in parts
TERRAIN: Hilly, fields, coast path, cycle path. Often muddy.
FOOTWEAR: Walking Boots. In dry weather trainers, etc. should be fine.
SUITABLE FOR: Good for dogs. Great views, local history, beach stop.
COWS / SHEEP/ HORSES: Cows likely - alternate route available
PARKING: Mevagissey Long Stay Car parks. Willow Carpark / Sunny Corner. PL26 6RZ
WCS: Mevagissey / Pentewan
CAFE / PUB: Mevagissey / Pentewan
OS MAP: 105

BRIEF DESCRIPTION: This is a great walk that follows the cycle path up towards Heligan. It then branches off across several fields with great views. The path then winds down into Pentewan, from there we follow the coast path home to Mevagissey taking in an abandoned set of pilchard stores. The last section is demanding.

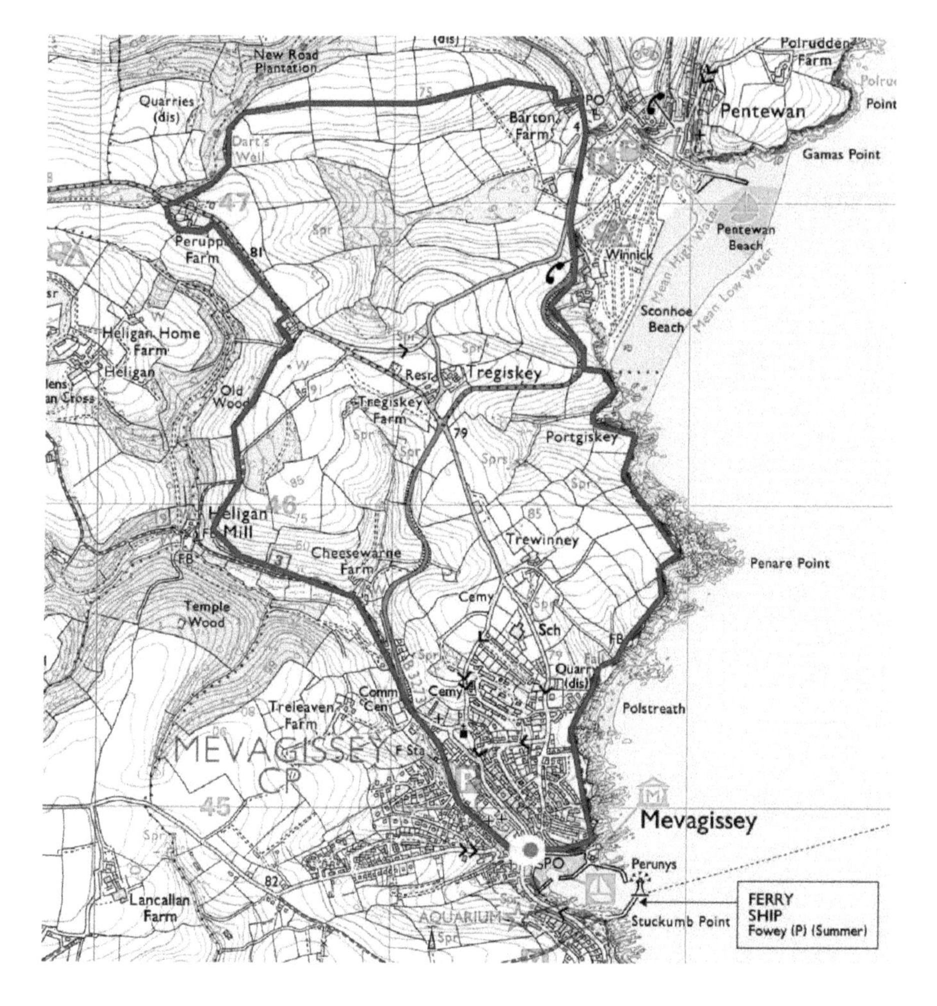

Elevation Profile

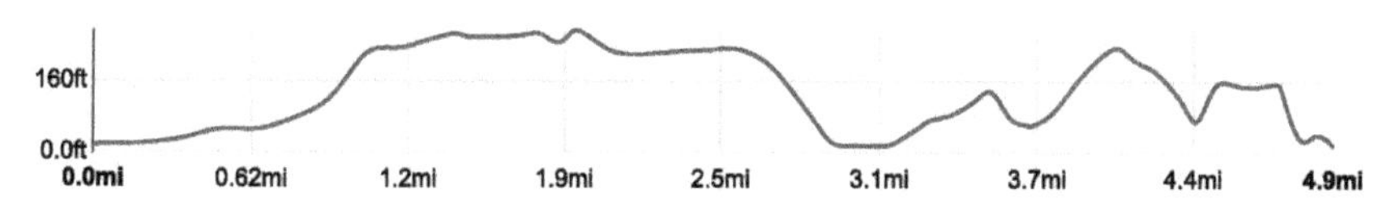

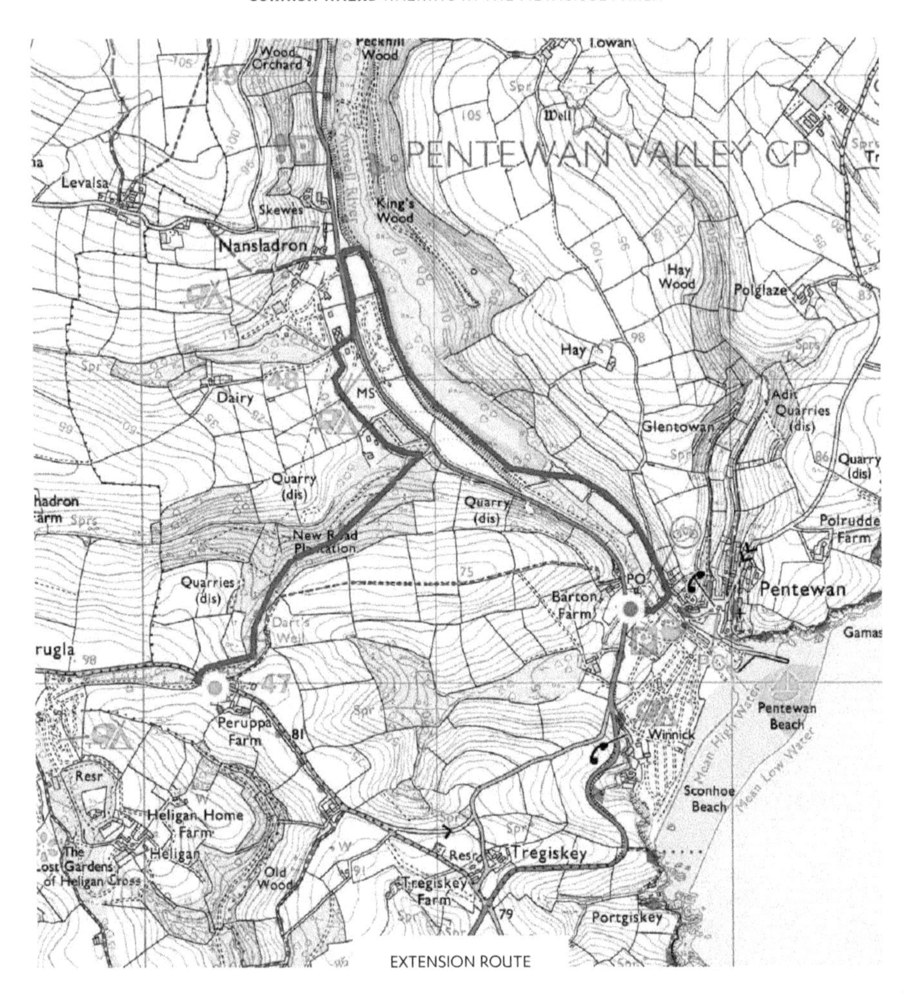

EXTENSION ROUTE

DIRECTIONS:

1. From your car park make your way onto the B3273, this is the main St Austell road leading out of the village. Head north in the St Austell direction. You will pass the bus stop and fire station, on your left, and as the road starts to head uphill, look to your left by the Mevagissey Community Centre. You will see signs to Heligan going via the National Cycle Path, route 3. Take this path.

2. Around your first mile, there is a footpath leading off towards Heligan; this is just as the cycle path turns right and starts to head uphill. Ignore this path and stay on the cycle trail for another mile. At first, there is a very steep section, and then the path levels out. After a while, the path will navigate an electricity sub-station, and the path will then run alongside a road. See *Heligan*.

3. It will then start to pass along a collection of old farm buildings. As you pass the buildings, the path will begin to rise again turning left, at the point of the second left-hand bend you will leave cycle route 3. From the end of the farm buildings to this junction is approximately 30 yards. Your new path is off to the right and is often overgrown and poorly signed. You need to find the tall metal post on the left, pointing to Mevagissey and Pentewan. Directly to the right is your path. If you find yourself at a T-junction and to your right you are looking at a stone road

Heligan: The Heligan Estate was first recorded in the 1200s, it was taken over by the Tremayne family, with the house that we see today, being built in the 1700s. The Estate grew and prospered until the state of the First World War. Then the Estate workers along with many from the village enlisted and went off to war.

The villages tended towards the Navy, but those from the Estate were land men and joined the army. The majority died, and the residing Tremayne owner moved to Italy, and the Estate fell into neglect. The house was split into flats in the seventies, but the gardens continued to be neglected until Tim Smit and John Wills, one of the Tremayne family, started to explore the grounds following the 1990 hurricane. They discovered the bones of a wonderful Victorian Estate, with many of the features still standing, just. Over the next few decades, it has been restored and turned into the nation's favourite garden, regularly voted by the nation's favourite public garden.

bridge, you have overshot the path. Head back, although from this direction the new footpath is easier to see.

(If you wish to take the longer route or avoid the potential cows in the field ahead, this is the point when you need to follow the alternative route. Go to step 13.)

ENJOY THE REST

4. This is a short path that leads to the road so if you are walking with a dog, it's best to have them on a lead. At the road, cross directly over towards the unmade lane. There is a footpath sign to the right of this unmade lane. Follow the old road down to a five-bar gate. Regardless of whether the gate is open or not, climb over the granite stile to the left of the gate. Take this path, turning right through the woods, it will follow the edge of the field and after 50 yards, climb over the granite stile to your right. You are now near the bottom of the field you just left. Continue along the edge of the field until you get to the bottom left edge of the next field.

5. The walk now continues through five arable fields. The path cuts diagonally through the middle of the first three fields. It can seem a bit unnerving at first, especially in the winter months where the path isn't clear but head forward on a diagonal path and as you climb the field you will see the gap in the hedgerow ahead, walk towards that. It is easier to see the gap in the hedge in the next two fields. During high summer the path is very clear,

but the views disappear as the crop, if corn, will be about 10 foot high. As you leave the third field, the path now follows along the right-hand edge of the field, with the hedge always on your right. Continue downhill into the fifth field, keeping the hedge on your right.

6. Dogs on lead for the next few stages. At the bottom of the field, there is a five-bar gate with a kissing gate to the left. There are usually cattle in the field. **Check the tips in the front of this book for walking through cattle.** The path is in the middle of the field and heads downhill and to the right. You are heading towards the large oak tree that you can see on your right as you pass through the gate. At the bottom of the field is another kissing gate that leads into an old drive heading down towards the B3273. Cross over towards the Mill Garage and then follow the main road right, heading towards Mevagissey.

(This is where the alternate route re-joins the walk.)

7. At this point, you can walk left into Pentewan for refreshments or a bit further on, turn left into Pentewan Sands, again for refreshments and a swim. Pentewan is the village. Pentewan Sands is a holiday park with a large sandy private beach. There is a dog ban for most of the year and no facilities in winter.

Portgiskey: There is a small collection of pilchard cellars. Pilchard fishing was the main industry of St Austell Bay. For reasons that are unclear the pilchard began to turn up in our waters in vast numbers. The whole of the St Austell Bay benefited from this bounty, but it was Mevagissey that was pre-eminent in the fishing industry. Although not particularly popular in Britain, the pilchard was highly sought after on the continent. At one point in the early 1900's, the St Austell Bay area exported around 75 million pilchards. To process the fish, they were first salted in brine tanks and then packaged in wooden casks. The casks had holes in the bottom, and a lid was placed on top to which weights were added in order to squeeze the oil from the fish. To further leverage the squeeze, a long pole was slotted into the hole in the wall, and weights were tied to the end of it. The pole rested on top of the lid and pressed the pilchard. The lids were then fitted, and the barrels were shipped out.

8. Little Bay Café offer free bottles of water on production of this walking guide. Details at the end of the walk

9. The path now continues along the coast path. This is picked up just by the right-hand side of the white entrance gates to Pentewan Sands. It is signed for the Coast Path. The path heads inland for a while and then the path splits. Take the left-hand path over the stile and now follow the path back to Mevagissey. Keep the sea on your left. If you find yourself on the footpath directly on the road, you have overshot the turning for the coast path.

10. As the path heads back towards the sea, there is an option to head down to a small cove called Portgiskey. It is also possible to access Portgiskey from Pentewan Sands, avoiding the hill path, but this is only possible at very low tide and may also involve some rock scrambling. **See *Portgiskey.***

11. The path then continues to Meva and is quite arduous, with lots of ups and downs, although it is only about a mile. As the path heads into Mevagissey, you will begin to pass some gardens to your right and a gate into Trevalsa Hotel on your right. Just after this, there is a path on your left down to Polstreath Beach. This is a lovely and often empty beach. Possibly because of the 100 steps.

12. Continuing along the coast path you start to look down on the harbour of Mevagissey, carry on down through the tiny lanes and then rest.

Pentewan: As you walk across the fields, to the right, you are looking over St Austell Bay and Pentewan. Pentewan was first mentioned in 1086 in the Domesday Book and has continued as a small working village. It has benefited from having a local quarry extracting Pentewan Stone, tin extraction from the local river, being a major port for the China Clay Industry with a railway line serving it from St Austell, and it has also been a home for fishing boats and the pilchard industry. Walking around the village, you will see many remnants of its long industrial heritage.

PENTEWAN SANDS

ALTERNATIVE ROUTE:

13. This adds an extra two miles but they are downhill and then flat. Do not leave the cycle path but continue on until you meet a T-junction, about 100 metres. Turn right and walk under the road bridge, follow this trail all the way down the hill. The cycle path follows the main road and then crosses over it. You will then follow the pavement for a few yards and then turn right over the river. Once you have crossed the bridge, turn right and walk downstream along the river. Take the large obvious left-hand path that leads into the woods. This will take you into Pentewan village. Pass the cycle hire shop and then you are back on a road. Turn right and walk along it until you get to the main road and the Mill Garage. At this point, you will re-join the original route at **Step 7. See *Pentewan.***

FRIENDLY LOCALS

LINKS:

http://heligan.com/the-story/introduction/

http://www.pentewan.com/a-brief-history-1/

http://www.cornwallgoodseafoodguide.org.uk/cornish-fishing/history-of-the-cornish-fishing-industry.php

https://www.tripadvisor.co.uk/Restaurant_Review-g2305614-d10194863-Reviews-Little_Bay_Cafe-Pentewan_St_Austell_Cornwall_England.html

PHOTO ALBUM:

https://www.flickr.com/photos/97473606@N04/albums/72157686207884561

4

MEVAGISSEY - GORRAN - GALOWRAS - PORTMELLON - MEVAGISSEY

LENGTH: 7 miles
EFFORT: Medium
TERRAIN: Coastal path, footpaths, lanes.
FOOTWEAR: Walking Boots. In dry weather trainers, etc. should be fine.
SUITABLE FOR: A good range of Cornish habitats, beach, streams, hills, fields, woods. Dogs on leads for the first section.
COWS / SHEEP / HORSES: Some potential.
PARKING: Mevagissey Long Stay Car parks. Willow Carpark / Sunny Corner. PL26 6RZ
WCS: Mevagissey / Gorran
CAFE / PUB: Mevagissey / Gorran / Gorran Haven
OS MAP: 105

BRIEF DESCRIPTION: An excellent walk taking in the coast path and then heading inland over fields and through woods. There are also lots of historic properties on view.

Elevation Profile

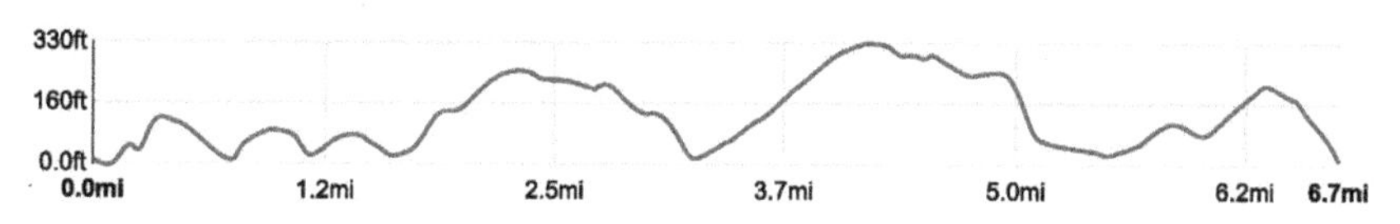

FULL INSTRUCTIONS

1. Start on Mevagissey's harbourside. From the harbour facing out to sea, walk to your right along the waterfront until you pass the tackle shop and just before the loos, take the steps up to Polkirt Hill. Walk uphill until you reach No.49, then take the footpath to your left. Continue to walk uphill. The footpath then splits, ahead to a large white building or right to re-join the road. For a nice detour, walk towards the white flats and through the gate, take the path onto the Crow's Nest for great views of the harbour and beyond.

2. Return to the path and head up to the road. The coast path now continues uphill along the road. This can be busy and tight in summer; drivers can be very frustrated at this point so please walk with care. As the road levels out there is a road turning downhill to the left called Portmellon Road, take this road all the way down into Portmellon, around the cove and back up out of the village. As you start heading uphill, and out of the village, take Chapel Point Lane on your left. Continue along as it becomes a private drive and after you have passed three benches look out for a sign to your left for the coast path and take it. See *Portmellon* and *Chapel Point*.

3. You are now on this path all the way to Gorran, traffic free. There will be some steps, stiles and sheep along the way as well as some steep cliffs. This section of the walk is about

Portmellon: Portmellon was the home to Percy Mitchell, a boat builder of high regard. His boatyard built hundreds of boats including boats sailed by Princess Elizabeth. He and his yard were considered the finest traditional boat builders in the country. As you walk, you can see the slipway that he built from his yard to launch the boats.

Chapel Point: Few builders left such an enduring mark on the area as architect John Archibald Campbell. The three houses at the end of Chapel Point were designed by him, and they are breath-taking examples of arts and craft architecture in the Scottish style. They were meant to be the forerunners of a Utopian housing project that he had successfully submitted plans for. Unfortunately one evening he walked off a cliff and died.

PENWARNE MANOR

two miles. Dogs will need to be on a lead for many sections of it. See *Bodrugan's Leap.*

4. As you drop into Gorran, the coast path joins a residential lane, follow all the little lanes downhill until you get to the beach at Gorran Haven.

5. From here with the beach behind you start to walk uphill on the main road on the left-hand side This is a long slow hill of about a mile up towards Gorran Churchtown. Ignore all turnings and footpaths until you get to a footpath sign on your left by the playing fields and a bench. (Ignore the one before heading to the school). Head over a very worn granite stile and cross the field diagonally to the break in the hedge. Over another old granite stile and continue diagonally to the field's corner and then re-join the road and turn left.

Bodrugan's Leap: So named because from here in 1487 it is said Sir Henry Bodrugan made a tremendous leap over the cliffs into a waiting boat and fled to France. He was being pursued by Sir Richard Edgecumbe for treason following the accession of Henry VII. Bodrugan was obviously a Yorkist. Following his leap from the cliffs, Henry Bodrugan became Cornwall's first recorded tombstoner!

Like most stories, it probably started with a grain of sand and became embellished. In a land of mermaids, giants and knockers, why should a man leaping successfully off a cliff be any less plausible?

LOW TIDE AT GORRAN HAVEN

GALOWRAS POND

6. After a few hundred yards the road veers sharply to the right, and there is a left-hand turning, at the junction, across the road, is a footpath taking you off the road. Take the footpath and follow it down to the village centre. As the footpath re-joins the road, you will pass a small donkey sanctuary on your left. The village stores and the Barley Sheaf Inn are just beyond the route, on your left, if you want to stop for refreshments.

7. The walk continues by taking the lane to the right, just before the Church. At the end of the church boundary, take the footpath labelled "Galowras Mill" to the left. The lane ends at three driveways, take the right-hand driveway to Cotna Barns and immediately walk across the lawn to the left, on a diagonal path heading towards a stile and a gap in the trees. Walk through the middle of the next field heading towards the break in the hedge. Head over this stile and now head off towards your right across the middle of the field. Once over the brow of the hill, you will see a small break in the trees and a very narrow stile. Head through into the woods. *See Domesday Land.*

8. The path now heads downhill very steeply. This is a grass path and likely to be very slippery in the wet. At the bottom of the hill, the path turns right and over a little stream. It now meanders along the edge of the valley floor with a large deciduous forest on the other side of the valley. The path gradually heads into the trees, at the

Domesday Land: Along with Bodrugan and Trevesson, Galowras is mentioned in the Domesday Book written in 1086, making these houses the remains of the oldest continuing settlements in this area.

Penwarne Manor: The manor dates back to the 13th century and was home to John Carew, son of the celebrated Cornish historian Richard Carew. John lost his hand in cannon fire at the Battle of Ostend in 1601. He was considered a fine and brave soldier, and clearly had a sense of humour as he brought the hand back to his landlady making a quip that it would be cutting no more puddings. This was a double jest, as puddings were often round like a cannonball and could be quite solid. Think Christmas pudding. John had a wooden arm fashioned and is one of the earliest recorded recipients of a prosthetic limb.

stile take the lower path and continue along the stream and ponds to your left. Eventually, you will come to a five-bar gate and a tiny lane. Turn left and follow the lane down towards Galowras Mill, cross the bridge and immediately take the footpath on the right. Head over two stiles, this section can be very muddy. Take the path around to the right, and you will come into a very large field on the side of a hill, there are often cattle in these fields but the fields are very large. Follow the path along to the right, through to the second field continue forward and as the path gets to the end of the field turn left and head to the top of the field. You can cross these two fields on their diagonal, but if there are cattle, you may feel happier sticking to the edges.

9. Cross the stile at the very top of the field and then follow the path down into the property of Penwarne Manor. Take the driveway to the right and head past the manor and uphill. Continue along the drive until it meets the Portmellon Park Road. Turn left uphill and where the road bends to the right take the footpath straight ahead. Ignore the first five-bar gate to your right and follow the lane up to until it ends at a five-bar gate. Go through this gate and turn right. Keep the hedgerow on your right, down to the kissing gate at the bottom of the two fields. The path now emerges onto Lower Well Park. Turn right and keep an eye out for a footpath sign after about 10 metres on the left. This path passes down between houses and comes out on Polkirt Hill. Turn left and head back down into Mevagissey. See *Penwarne Manor*.

CHAPEL POINT

LINKS:

https://nmmc.co.uk/object/people/percy-mitchell-a-traditional-boat-builder-par-excellence/

PHOTO ALBUM:

https://www.flickr.com/photos/97473606@N04/albums/72157686207884491

5

KING'S WOOD

LENGTH: 4 miles
EFFORT: One long hill. The rest is easy.
TERRAIN: Woodland, cycle path. Often muddy.
FOOTWEAR: Walking Boots. In dry weather trainers, etc. should be fine.
SUITABLE FOR: Excellent for dogs. Off lead the whole time, if desired, with a stream to clean off in, at the end. Part of the path is shared with a cycleway; leads may be required.
COWS / SHEEP/ HORSES: None.
PARKING: King's Wood PL26 6DJ This is the closest postcode. Not exact.
TOILETS: Pentewan
CAFE / PUB: Pentewan
OS MAP: 105

BRIEF DESCRIPTION: A sheltered woodland and river stroll.

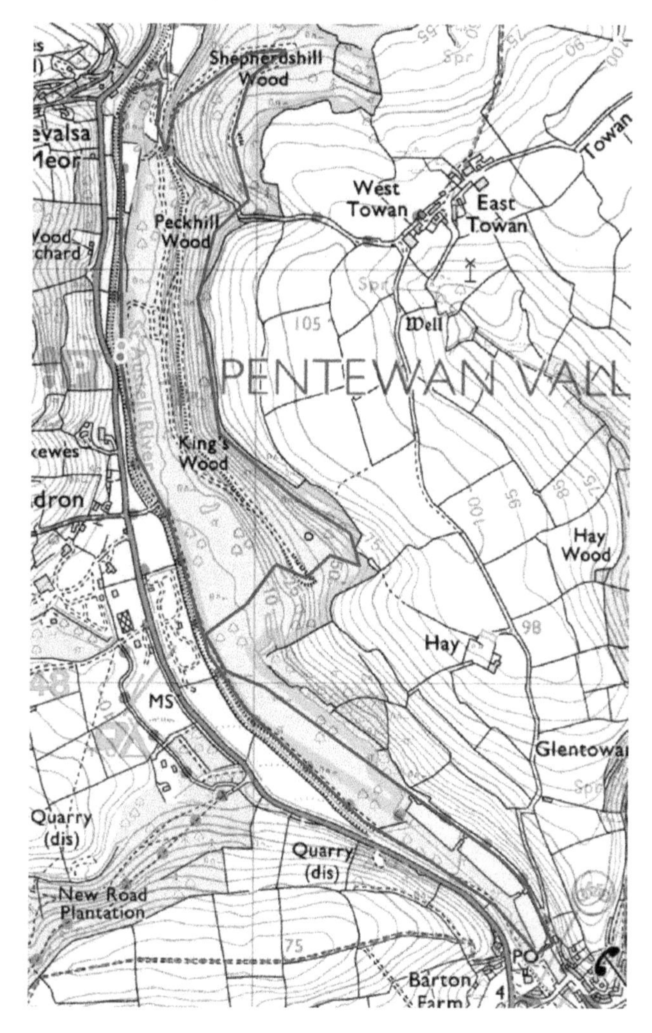

Elevation Profile

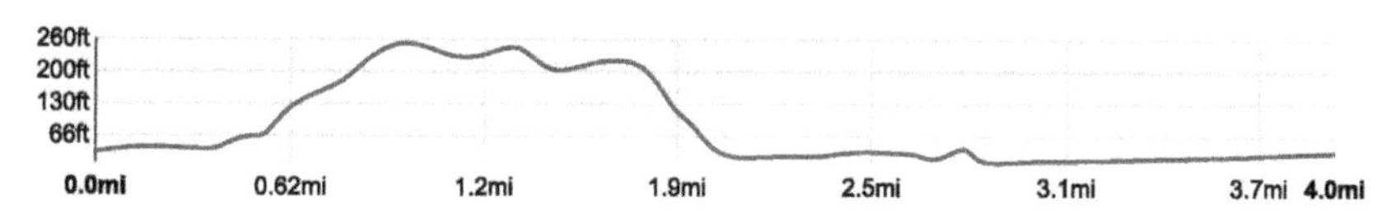

DIRECTION:

1. For this first section, you may want to keep any dogs on a lead if they aren't good with bikes. Equally the path crosses a small road.

2. From the car park (not the lay-by), looking towards the main road, take the right-hand path and walk upstream, along the river. Follow this path in through the woods and over a small bridge until it joins a larger unmade road. Turn right and head up into the car park/clearing. *See King's Wood.*

3. You now have a choice of two paths that rejoin each other after a short while.

OPTION ONE

Within the clearing are three exits. Go through the kissing gate by the five-bar gate to the left of the car park. Follow the path uphill, after about five minutes the path turns sharply to the right, almost back on itself. It is still the principle path so ignore any other left or right-hand turns. The path ends at a large open clearing with several exits. You are heading for the top left exit by the bench. The path goes uphill into the wood.

Follow the path as it dips down to the right, up again and then it heads downhill, through the pine trees, veering left. At the edge of a steep ridge looking down, the path becomes difficult to see. You need to be walking on a compass bearing of around 150 degrees SSE.

King's Wood: At one point in its history, the woodland was thought to be a designated deer park. If you look at the very fine retaining wall at the very highest point of the walk, you will see that it was constructed with over-capped stones, presumably to stop deer leaping out.

OLD TRACKWAYS

FAIRY DOOR

There are some steps cut into the hillside, and they swing around to 210 degrees SSW. Keep heading SW, and the final few steps will end at a Woodland Trust post. The path then meets the old road mentioned in Option Two. Turn left and walk uphill for a few metres until you see the path off to the right of the road, marked by another Woodland Trust post.

(If you lost the path coming down through the trees, you will need to re-navigate yourself up or down the old road accordingly, until you find the Woodland Trust post.)

OPTION TWO

To the left and right are five-bar gates, in between, and in front of you is the continuation of the old road. It is very atmospheric but also very steep. Towards the top of the hill and just before the road turns sharply to the left, you turn right and follow the Woodland Trust post.

This is where the two options join.

4. Stepping off the old road by the Woodland Trust post, turn left uphill towards the sky, following the intermittent steps. You should now be walking in a SW direction with a stone wall to your left and fields beyond the wall. Follow this path for about a mile. After roughly three-quarters of a mile, and just after a bench, the path turns right and begins to head steeply downhill. It zigs once,

Pentewan Refreshments: Pentewan is well worth a visit and has a great pub, cafe,loos and beach. Little Bay cafe offer free bottles of water on production of this guide. Their location is in the links section at the end of this walk. They are just by the pub.

sharp right and then zags sharp left at a Trust post. The path now veers right but splits into two paths at the tree with a red fairy door at the base of its trunk. Take the left-hand path and continue downhill.

5. The path heads over a stream bed and just after the stream on your right is the remnants of a woodlander's cottage. The path turns right and continues downhill until it opens into another large grass clearing. You now need to take the path off to the left, marked by another post. Head back into the wood and downhill, as the path levels out it turns left towards a small wooden bridge crosses a stream.

6. Head over the footbridge and bear right, through the beech and oak trees. Keep any posts you see to your right and head down to your left towards a stream and a series of causeways and small wooden bridges. This section of the valley floor is often very wet and or muddy. The path through is clear until the second last causeway when it seems to stop, the final causeway bridge is about 70 steps away in a SW direction. You may need to weave about a bit to find a non-muddy section.

7. Once on the causeway walk towards the edge of the wood. You now pop out onto the cycle track alongside the White River. *See St Austell River or White River.*

Pentewan: Pentewan was first mentioned in 1086 in the Domesday Book and has continued as a small working village. It has benefited from having a local quarry extracting Pentewan Stone, tin extraction from the local river, being a major port for the China Clay Industry with a railway line serving it from St Austell, and it has also been a home for fishing boats and the pilchard industry. If you choose to walk around the village, you will see many remnants of its long industrial heritage.

St Austell River or White River: Along the valley floor of this river, it was used for tin streaming, a way to catch tin deposits floating downstream. In more recent centuries the river changed colour from red to white. As the China Clay was extensively mined in the St Austell region, the whole area including the rivers turned white as they carried the runoff. In heavy rain, the sea itself would turn white where a river ran into it. Even today, in very heavy rain the river will turn a milky colour.

8. From here on the navigation is easy. Turn left and follow the river, downstream, after about a hundred yards the large path turns left back into the woods. Stay on this path for about half a mile until just after a dog bin, and just before you reach the Cycle Hire Centre at Pentewan. See *Pentewan* and *Pentewan Refreshment*.

9. Continuing the walk, return to this point. There is now a right-hand turning by the dog bin. Take this path to the river's edge and turn right. You now walk upstream all the way back to your car, roughly a mile away.

BEYOND THE PATH LIE THE REMAINS OF TIN STREAMING

LINKS:

Tin Streaming http://www.historic-cornwall.org.uk/flying-past/streams.html

https://www.woodlandtrust.org.uk/visiting-woods/wood-information/kings-wood/

https://www.tripadvisor.co.uk/Restaurant_Review-g2305614-d10194863-Reviews-Little_Bay_Cafe-Pentewan_St_Austell_Cornwall_England.html

PHOTO ALBUM:

https://www.flickr.com/photos/97473606@N04/albums/72157686207884511

6

GRAMPOUND - CREED - GOLDEN MILL - TREWITHEN - GRAMPOUND

LENGTH: 5 miles.
EFFORT: Easy
TERRAIN: Mostly country lanes. Some fields (avoidable) and tracks
FOOTWEAR: General
SUITABLE FOR: All. A lot of this walk is on lanes so suitable for buggies, but some of the footpaths are bumpy. Terrain buggy only.
COWS / SHEEP/ HORSES: Cows but avoidable.
PARKING: TR2 4RT
WCS: Grampound Community Centre
CAFE / PUB: Grampound Community Centre / The Dolphin Arms
OS MAP: 105

BRIEF DESCRIPTION: A nice easy walk through country lanes, discovering little hamlets and fine country houses. This walks spans every historic age of Cornwall with evidence of Iron age hillforts and Roman settlements as well as Domesday properties and medieval barns.

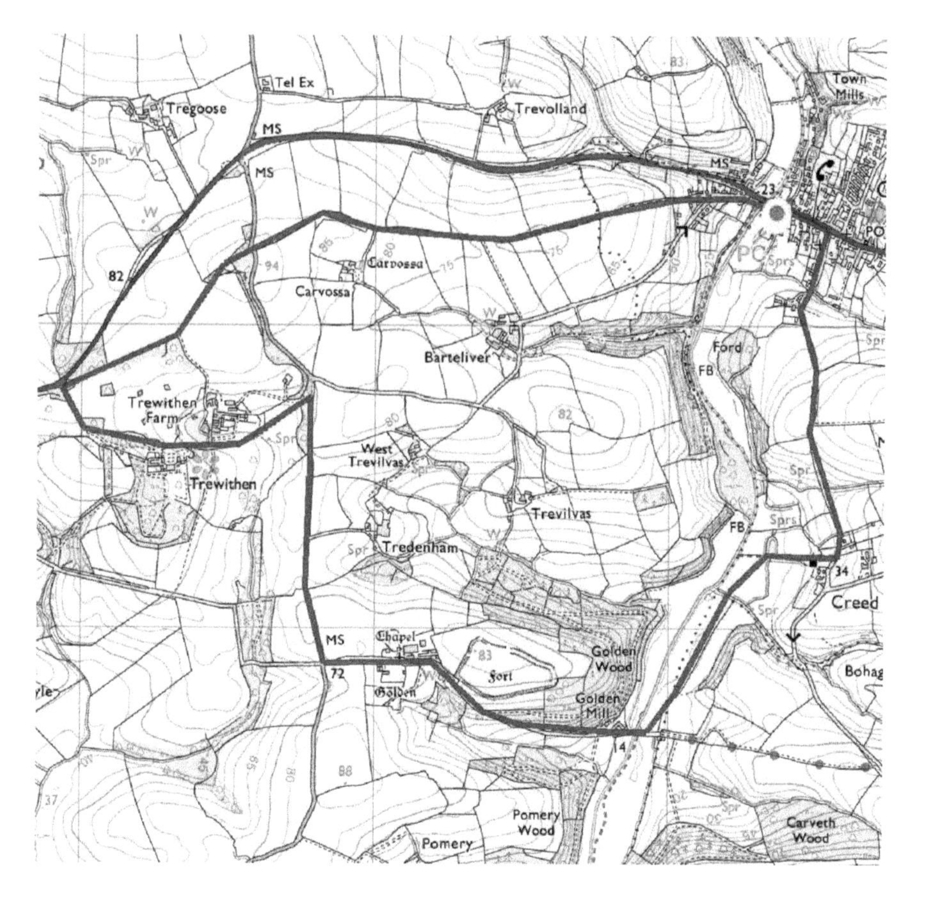

Elevation Profile

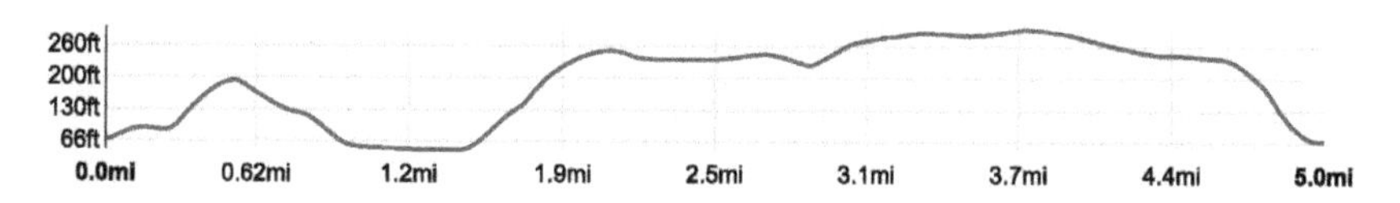

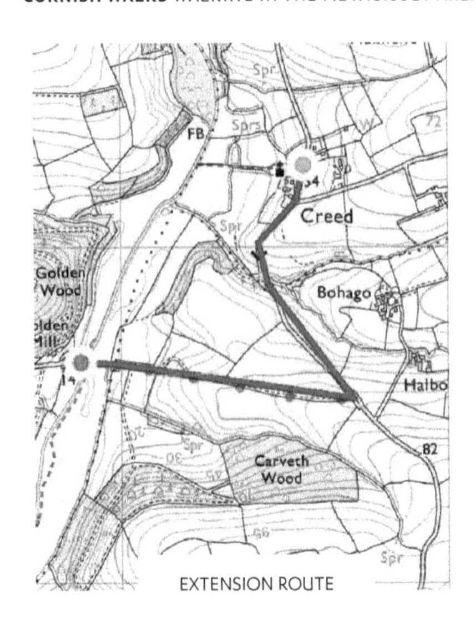

EXTENSION ROUTE

DIRECTIONS:

1. From the Grampound car park, head towards the main road and turn right, walk along the road until you get to the turning on the right for Creed. Walk along this lane for just under a mile. After a quarter of a mile keep a look out for the remains of a medieval stone cross in the hedgerow on your left. All that is now left is the base and a hole where the upright would have stood, making it look like a well. This was one of a series of crosses linking Grampound and Creed. Continue along the road until you get the Creed. When you get to the main Church gates on your right, you now have two options. The next section of the path is permissive and closed between Oct and Mar for the shooting season. There are also normally a lot of cows in the fields ahead. **See *Grampound*.**

Grampound: This has long been the site of an important settlement, from the Iron Age Hillfort, the Roman Settlement, the Domesday parish and the Mediaeval market to a Georgian and Victorian commercial centre. Sitting at the junction of one of Cornwall's principal routes with its great bridge providing the first crossing point over the River Fal, Grampound has a long and established history. Just in front of St Nun's Church stands an impressive medieval cross. Hidden behind the main road and now redeveloped as homes, lies the site of Grampound Tannery, home to the highly sought after, Croggon leather.

OPTION ONE.

Avoiding fields. Continue walking along the road. Head uphill for about half a mile and the take an unmade road to you right. Ignore the track by the river and continue uphill. (If you get as far as the left-hand road junction you have just overshot the pathway.) There are lovely views from this high road, to your right you can just see Creed Church and ahead you can see a wood sheltering Golden Camp, an Iron Age hill fort. You can see why such a spot was chosen, it must have had great views. It also sat above the River Fal, which was much wider and deeper than today. Now continue along the road, eventually, it will drop down and you will get to the River Fal. This is the where Option Two joins the path. **See *Creed Church*.**

OPTION TWO.

Closed October – March. Go through the church gates and take the path on the left of the church, follow the path down to the fence on the left and then leave the churchyard. The path now goes through a spinney, for about 200 yards, it can be overgrown. The path now drops down to the left and over a small wooden bridge that spans a little stream. You are now in the first of two fields. The metal wires you need to duck under are electrified. It will give you a small tingle if you touch it. Head across the middle of the field to the gap in the hedge. You are now in a very long field, walk the length of it until you get to a five-bar gate at the other end. There are often cows in these fields. If your way is blocked by cattle you can take the footbridge over the River Fal into the next field and continue left towards the five-bar gate at the end of this field. (This is not the proper path, but if you suddenly need to avoid the cattle, it's an option.) Once you have left the field you are at the same point as the alternative option.

2. Cross over the Fal via the road bridge, and take the road uphill. There is a "pub" to your right but you won't get a drink here, it's a private building for the Estate Shoots. Walking on, you pass through the lovely hamlet of Golden and eventually reach a T-junction. From the River Fal to this T-Junction is about half a mile. Turn right and continue for another half a mile. This road can be busy so watch out for traffic as there are no pavements. After half a mile, take the left-hand turning into the grounds of Trewithen Estate. Stick to the main drive through the Estate passing the lake on your right and after a while Trewithen House itself on the

left. If the gardens and cafe are open, this is a nice place to stop and explore. Trewithen is generally only opened in the Spring. **See *Golden* and *Trewithen Estate*.**

3. Continue along the main drive as it heads out to the main road. Pass through the Estate gate posts and cattle grid and then directly to your right you will see a white picket fence and a gate, go through the gate.

4. You are now walking along what is considered to be a Roman road. This bridleway will take you back to the start of the walk. Like any good Roman road, this is a pretty straight path. Every time the path seems to turn to the right ignore it and continue forward. Each of the right turns have Private signs, so you don't need to worry about getting lost. The path starts on grass, goes through a small copse, then crosses a minor road. There is no more traffic, after this point, and the path travels between fields. After you have crossed the road, the next turning on the right is towards a house called Carvossa. This is also the location of a Romano British site, Caerfos, archaeology shows a settlement from 60 AD to the third century. Nothing is visible. When the path starts to head down the hill and under trees, you may want to get any dogs back on lead as you are about to head back into Grampound village. The path re-joins a village lane that heads down towards the main Truro road. Turn right and walk along the main road, over the river, and then back to where you parked your car.

Creed Church: Some Norman construction can be seen but the majority of the Church is from the 14th to 16th century, and it has good examples of mediaeval stained glass. In 1791 the Rector of Creed, William Gregor, discovered Titanium. Details of the discovery on the Lizard, are in the Church.

Golden: A very small but pretty hamlet, consisting of a farm, a well, a manor house and some very old buildings incorporated into the farm. The building that looks like a chapel might be part of the old manor house and dates from around the sixteenth century.

Trewithen Estate: A large family home with Spring opening only. John Hawkins was the first member of the family to move to the county in 1554. Originally a courtier to Henry VIII, he settled at Trewinnard, near St Erth, married and established a maritime trading business through Mevagissey that thrived for many years. The current house was built in the seventeenth century.

SUNSET OVER CARVOSSA

LINKS

https://www.geocaching.com/geocache/GC6FC58_golden-chapel?guid=4a5994a6-2c5a-4b6a-b884-c350fe91f910

https://trewithengardens.co.uk/ https://historicengland.org.uk/listing/the-list/list-entry/1016890

PHOTO ALBUM:

https://www.flickr.com/photos/97473606@N04/albums/72157686207884601

7

POLGOOTH - NANSLADRON - POLGOOTH

LENGTH: 4.5 Miles
EFFORT: Moderate
TERRAIN: Mixed terrain; fields, paths, roads. Some paths can be very muddy to the extent of spoiling the walk. Better in dry weather.
FOOTWEAR: Walking boots / trainers.
SUITABLE FOR: Walkers only. Dogs on lead for many sections.
COWS / SHEEP/ HORSES: Cows and sheep very likely.
PARKING: The Polgooth Inn*. PL26 7DA
WCS: The Polgooth Inn*
CAFE / PUB: The Polgooth Inn*
OS MAP: 105

BRIEF DESCRIPTION: A nice countryside stroll taking in some industrial archaeology and ending at an excellent pub.

**If parking at the pub, please leave a sign in your window. My thanks to The Polgooth Inn for allowing us to use their car park. Pop in for a drink or some food, you won't be disappointed.*

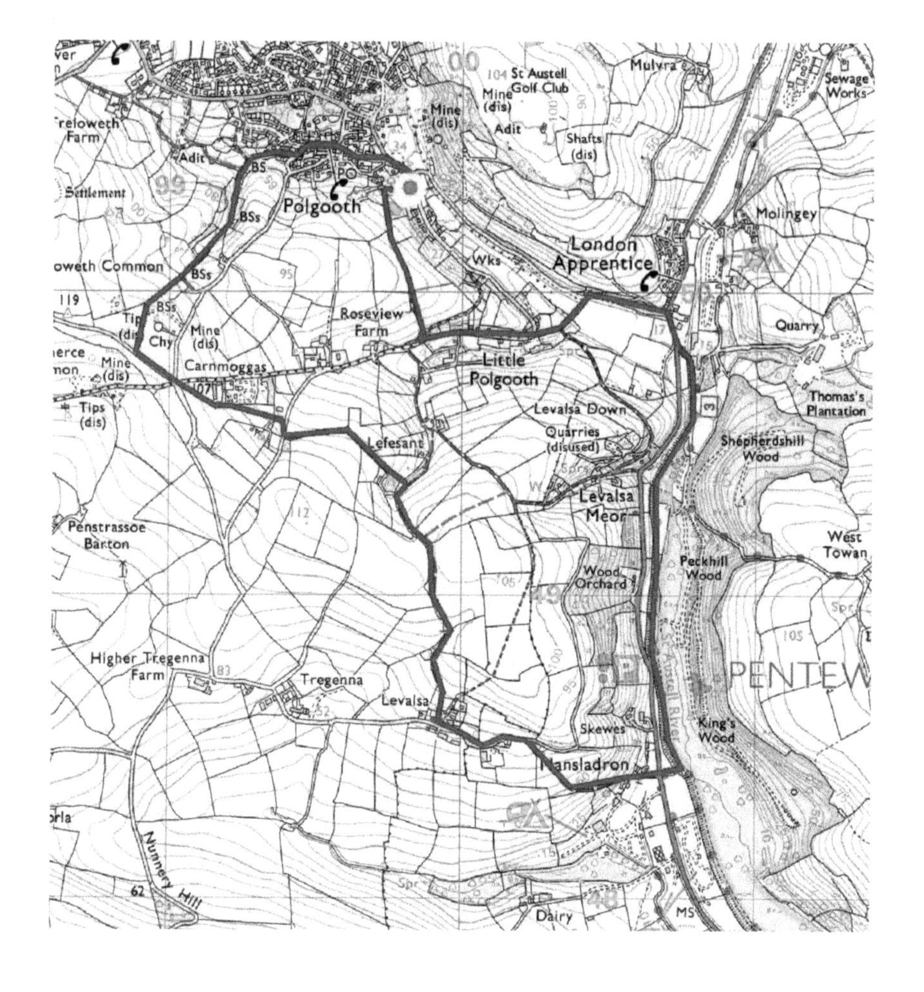

Elevation Profile

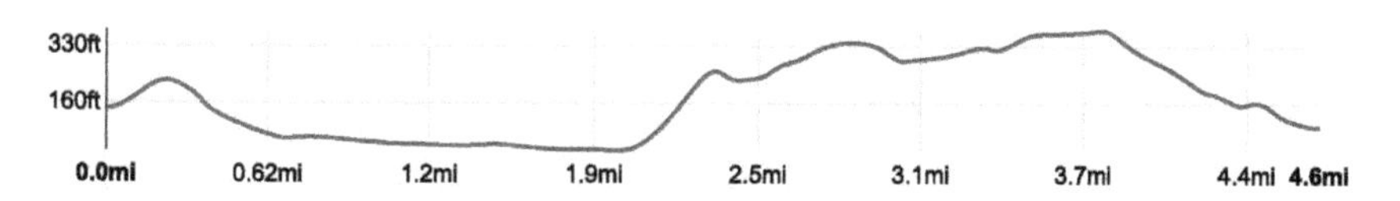

DIRECTIONS:

1. From the pub car park, take the track to the right of the pub,nthat leads uphill. This is a wide track and looks bit like a private driveway. Climb the path until it meets a T-junction, turn left. Follow this path up and over the hill until it drops down onto a tarmacked road. Turn left. The next few roads are small but often busy so take care, there are no pavements.

2. Walk along the road until you get to the next T-junction. Turn right and follow the road down to the main road. Now cross over towards The Kingswood Restaurant and walk right. Take the turning left, off the main road, towards a small industrial estate. Walk past the estate turnings and towards the trail and parking area. You are now on the Pentewan Valley Trail. Take the path right; this is a shared use trail, so watch out for other traffic. Follow the trail until just as it starts to turn uphill towards another car parking area. Just before the hill the trail turns right and is signposted Pentewan Trail 3, follow the path through the woods and towards the river. Continue along the river bank downstream. The path passes another car park and then continues along the river. When you get to a bridge, cross over. This is not the bridge by the car park. Following the path over the bridge, you come to a main road. Directly ahead of you is a drive, cross the road and walk up the drive, there is a small house sign on the left saying "Coachman's

Polgooth: Antiquarians once claimed that the mines of Polgooth had supplied Phoenician traders with tin 3000 years ago, but in fact, the earliest historical record is a list compiled in 1593, in which several well-established Polgooth workings were named. At that time and subsequently, the mines were owned by the Edgcumbe family.

By 1803, Polgooth was celebrated as the "greatest tin mine in the world" and the richest mine in the United Kingdom. The village of Polgooth grew up amongst the mines. In 1824, a travel guide by FWL Stockdale noted that "The whole surface of the country in this vicinity, has been completely disfigured, and presents a very gloomy aspect...The immense piles of earth, which have been excavated and thrown up, have quite a mountainous appearance: roads have been formed in several directions leading to the places or shafts, where the miners are at work; and the dreariness of the scene is only enlivened by the humble cottages, which have been erected for their residence."

We can still see this today, the cottages are in haphazard arrangements, growing up between the mines, placed on the side of a

Cottage" go up between the houses, when you get to "Higher Nansladron" leave the drive and take the path straight ahead, and continue uphill. This path is very unven and get be slippy in the wet.

3. At the top of the path go through the five-bar gate and into a field. Walk forwards, with the hedge on your left, for about twenty metres., The path now cuts diagonally uphill and to the right through the middle of the field. Your exit is just below the house that will become visible as you climb the field. This field regularly has cattle in it. If you need to take an alternate route across the field to get to the exitpoint that is fine. As you go through this gate, you are in the garden of a private home. Stick to the left-hand side of the path and out through the gate at the end of their drive.

4. Walk along the road until you get to the impressive Levalsa Farmhouse on the right. Take the concrete drive on your right, just past the farmhouse. Go up the drive and as it turns right, take the path that splits off it, by the metal gate. At one point the path turns into more of a track and there is a five-bar gate to your left, continue up the track as it bends to the right. Eventually, the path ends at a five-bar gate, take the side gate and walk into the field ahead. Follow the field boundary to the left, stay following the field edge until you get to a gate and stile.

valley between leats and streams. Now added to the village are lots of bungalows and chalets, and the whole village has an alpine feel to it.

ONE OF THE HIDDEN TRACKWAYS

SOUTH POLGOOTH MINE

5. Leave the field here and head down the track. **Your next turning is easy to miss.** As you pass a drive and gateway on your left, you continue downhill for about 100 metres, then on your left-hand side, the path steps off. There are a few stone steps visible on the track's edge. If you pass a dwelling on the left, you have overshot the path. The following half-mile can become very difficult in wet condition due to extreme mud and flooded lanes.

(If you are not in suitable footwear consider this diversion. As you walk down the track stay on it until it reaches the main road. There is no footpath on this road and can be busy. At the main road, turn left. Walk uphill for about a half mile, at one point the road splits, take the right-hand spilt until you get to the Fiveways junction. Resume the walk at point 8.)

6. The path cuts across a boggy area and up through a small stream for a few footsteps. The path is now clear, leading up between two fields and is often very claggy. The path turns into a small track that can have some very large puddles, eventually, the track ends at a road.

7. Turn right and after about 30 metres take the footpath on your left, opposite a pylon. There is a footpath sign and a five-bar gate. Follow the path up for a few metres, and take the wooden stile on your right. The path now cuts upwards through a field and your exit is at the top right. There are often sheep in this field. As you walk through the field there is a caravan park to your right and, as you crest the field, South Polgooth Mine ahead.

8. As you leave the field via the five-bar gate, you are at the road junction called Five Ways, for obvious reasons. This is where the alternative route re-joins the walk.

9. There is now the option to explore the Engine House or to continue with the walk. If you explore the Engine House you will be directed to join the walk further on.

VISTING THE ENGINE HOUSE

From the Five Ways cross road, take the road signed towards Sticker. Follow the road for 200 metres until you get to a five bar gate on your right. This is a permissive path and could be removed by the farmer at any time. Squeeze around the gate post if the gate is locked. (Locked to prevent fly-tippers, not to prevent access). Walk towards the mine buildings and have a look around but take note that these are historic monuments and are potentially unsafe structures. There are two ways to leave the site. If you continue along the track you walked in on, you pass the buildings on your right and come to some arable fields. Directly to the right of the entrance to the field is a narrow path that runs between the field and a pasture. Head down the path and over the stile at the end. This is where the walks rejoin each other. This is the Black Path on the map insert.

Sometimes though, this path is heavily overgrown to the point of being impassable and invisible. If this is the case, return to the buildings and walk alongside the pasture, with the buildings on your right. Climb over a five bar gate, not the one you came in on, and head left, downhill on the road. You are now on the Polgooth Road as described in the section for avoiding the Engine House. This is the Red Path on the map inset.

AVOIDING THE ENGINE HOUSE

From the Five Ways cross road, take the road signed towards Polgooth. This is the Blue Path on the map inset.

10. Follow this road for around 300 metres until you see the signed footpath on your left. Take this bridleway, and it will end at a T-junction with a stile to the left. This is the stile that you climbed over if the path was navigable from the Engine House.

11. Now, turn right into the heavily covered path, (or straight ahead if you are coming from the Engine House) this old bridleway heads north into Polgooth village and also acts as a parish boundary. Several of the boundary stones are still visible. Keep walking forward on the path ignoring any left or rights until it gets to a residential lane. See *Polgooth.*

12. Polgooth is a very interesting village, in that it was created haphazardly and has not changed much. This means, that as you enter this side of the village, the lanes are incredibly higgledy-piggledy. It is almost impossible to tell you which path to take properly as there are no signs so, head downhill and right. This is a very small village so you really won't get lost. Keep the village stores on your right, then when you get to the Antique shop on your right, head forward and the Polgooth Inn will be ahead of you after about 200 metres. If in doubt, ask, everyone can tell you where the pub is.

ENGINE HOUSE MAP INSET

LINKS:

https://www.mindat.org/loc-209163.html

PHOTO ALBUM:

https://www.flickr.com/photos/97473606@N04/albums/72157688701409606

8

DODMAN POINT

LENGTH: 2.5 miles
EFFORT: Easy
TERRAIN: Coastal path, footpath
FOOTWEAR: Trainers / walking boots
SUITABLE FOR: Views and beach. Historic features.
COWS / SHEEP/ HORSES: Possible
PARKING: NT Car park at Penare. PL26 6NY Approach from the Gorran side, not the Boswinger side. The road is small and narrow from Gorran but it's much worse from Boswinger!
TOILETS: None (nearest Gorran Haven)
CAFE / PUB: None (nearest Gorran Haven)
OS MAP: 105

BRIEF DESCRIPTION: A lovely short loop heading along a track and onto the coastal path. Passing Dodman Point and then onto Hemmick Beach.

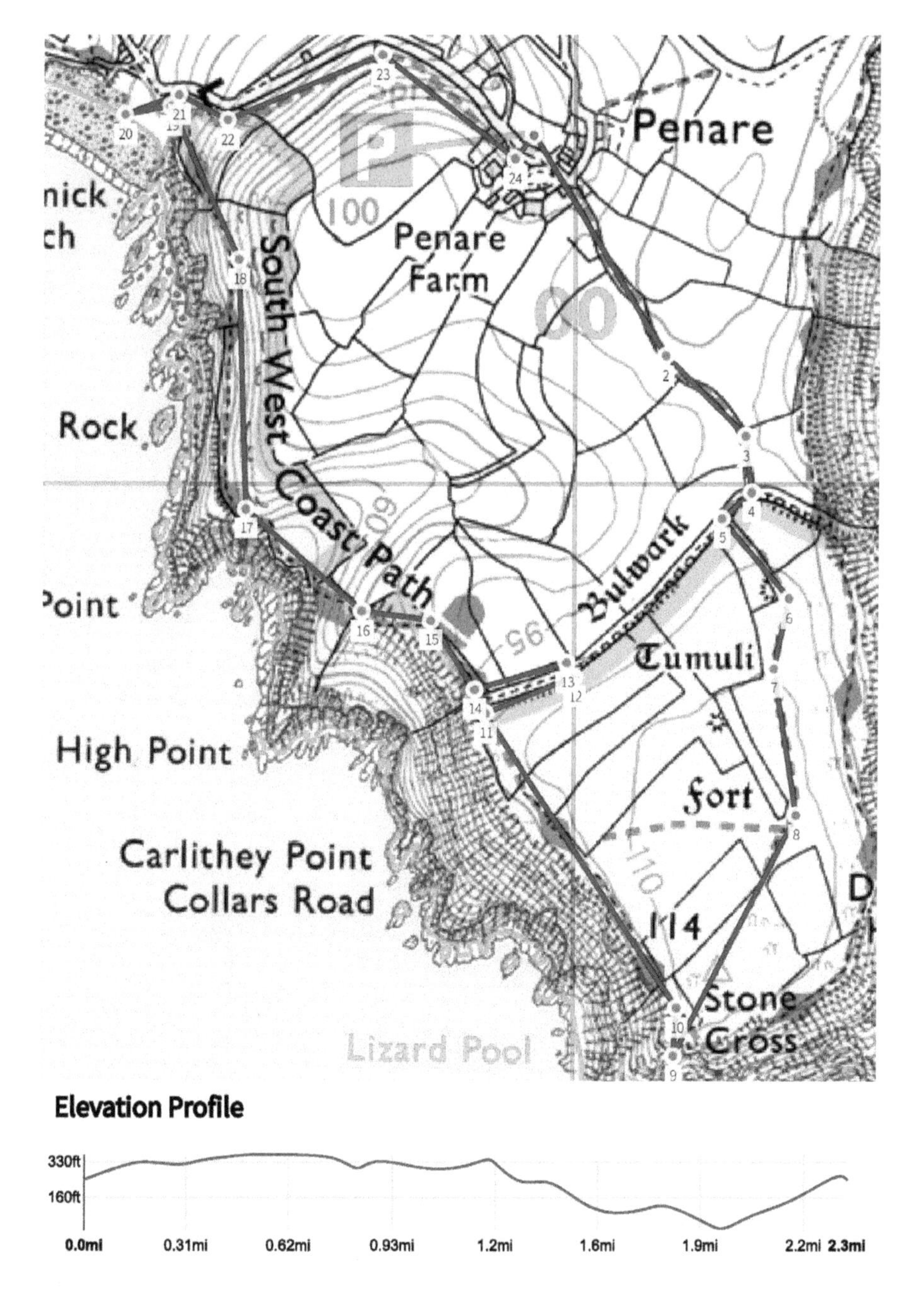
Penare
Penare Farm
South-West Coast Path
Rock
High Point
Carlithey Point
Collars Road
Bulwark
Tumuli
Fort
114
Stone Cross
Lizard Pool
100
95
110
Elevation Profile
330ft
160ft
0.0mi
0.31mi
0.62mi
0.93mi
1.2mi
1.6mi
1.9mi
2.2mi
2.3mi

DIRECTIONS:

1. From the car park, head up the road and take the footpath directly ahead, ignore the one to the right. Go through the five-bar gate and follow the track along to its end at another fire bargate. Go through the gate. You now have two options.

OPTION ONE.

Coast path, minor likelihood of seeing cattle.

Take the kissing gate ahead and slightly to your left. Follow this path down to the coast path and then turn right. Looking down and behind you is Vault Beach and the House above it is Lamledra. Walking along the coast path, with the sea on your left, you head onto the Dodman Point and the very large Cross. **See *Dodman Point*.**

Dodman Point: Also known as Deadman's Point, this small headland holds a wealth of historical features

A huge granite cross was placed here in 1896 as a navigational aid to seafarers. Opposite the path to the cross, you can take a short diversion inland to the watch-house, a 1795 survivor of a series of Admiralty signal stations used to alert the Navy at Plymouth.

In the fields behind the cross, there are a whole range of archaeological features. These include a later prehistoric cliff castle, the very impressive Bulwarks, with two prehistoric round barrows, and a mediaeval field system, situated on Dodman Point, a prominent flat-topped headland projecting south into the English Channel, south-west of Gorran Haven. Also within the scheduled area are a mediaeval or later trackway and beacon, a Napoleonic signal station, a building, extraction pits, a field system, boundary stones and a cross of the 18th and 19th centuries, and two probable World War II bomb craters.

THE DODMAN CROSS

OPTION TWO.

Through the fields. Much higher chance of cattle.

Turn right and walk along the footpath. After a short distance take the footpath on the left. There is a left and right spur, ignore the left-hand spur leading to a five-bar gate but take the right-hand spur instead and follow the path up between two hedges and then over the stile at the end. Once in the field follow the hedge on your right and when the hedge takes a right-hand turn continue walking forward across the middle of the field to the far right corner. Pass through the kissing gate and head towards the Napoleonic Lookout. Then head on to the Cross.

2. Having stood at the Cross return to the coast path and walk along with the sea still on your left. Carry along the coast path until you see a footpath signed to Penare on your right. Just before this, there is a V shape stile that will take you up onto the very impressive cliff castle ramparts. **WARNING**. There are some very large rabbit holes along this ridge concealed by the overgrowth. Walk with care.

3. The view up here is fabulous, and it is an incredible structure, to still be standing thousands of years later. At the end of this section, make your way back down to the path, this can be tricky, and then take the path back to the coast path.

Etymology: The Dodman Point is the highest point on the south coast of Cornwall at 374 feet. What does it mean? Who knows, but it really isn't likely to mean Deadman, despite the excited claims of some guides. Looking back over old texts and maps you can see that it was originally called Dudman. Dud is an archaic word for tattered clothes, maybe a joke about how windy it was up there?

Dudman Foreland, 1538; Dudman Poynt, 1579; Dudman Poynt, 1646; Dudman Poynt, 1678; Deadman Point, 1750; Dodman Point, 1811 and onwards. Further mentions of Deadman are simply ghoulish embellishments.

Hemmick Beach: Hemmick is a wonderful beach. There *may* be many better in Cornwall, but this is where my children grew up playing, so it is, in my opinion, the best beach in the world. Clear bias aside, it is a quiet beach, with great rock pools at low tide and a large sandy beach for games and adventures. No facilities.

4. Continue along the coast path until you drop down onto Hemmick Beach. **See *Hemmick Beach*.**

5. From the beach, head back the way you came this time taking the path that follows the road up. At the top of the hill, you will return to the car park.

OVERLOOKING THE DODMAN

LINKS

https://historicengland.org.uk/listing/the-list/list-entry/1020865

http://archaeologydataservice.ac.uk/archiveDS/archive-Download?t=arch-1062-1/dissemination/pdf/cornwall2-215495_1.pdf

PHOTO ALBUM:

https://www.flickr.com/photos/97473606@N04/albums/72157685450367322

9

SOUTH WEST COAST PATH PENTEWAN - PORTLOE

LENGTH: 14 miles
EFFORT: Strenuous
TERRAIN: Coastal path
FOOTWEAR: Walking boots
COWS / SHEEP/ HORSES: Possible
PARKING: Pentewan. However, this is a long walk to do there and back in a day. I would recommend booking a taxi at Portloe or a friend to pick you up. Portloe is on a Truro bus route 51
TOILET: Pentewan, Mevagissey, Gorran, Caerays, Portholland (seasonal), Portloe
CAFE / PUB: Pentewan, Mevagissey, Gorran, Caerays, Portholland (seasonal), Portloe
OS MAP: 105

BRIEF DESCRIPTION: A demanding but very scenic stretch of coastline; sandy beaches, smuggling coves, fishing harbours, stately homes and gardens, ancient hill forts and the highest point on the South Cornwall coastline.

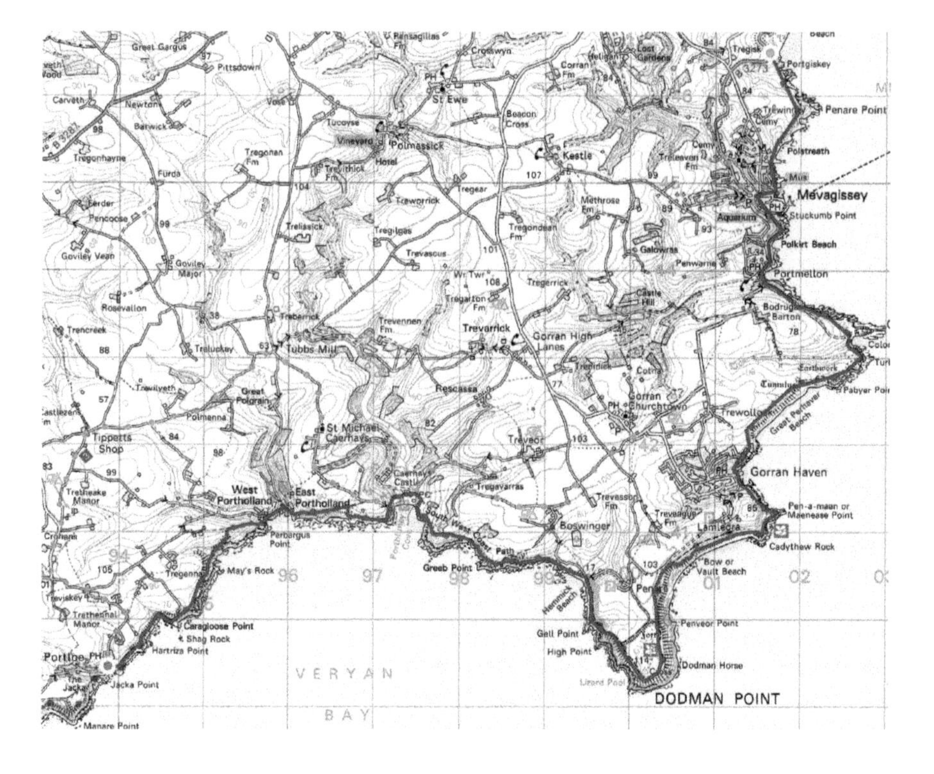

Elevation Profile

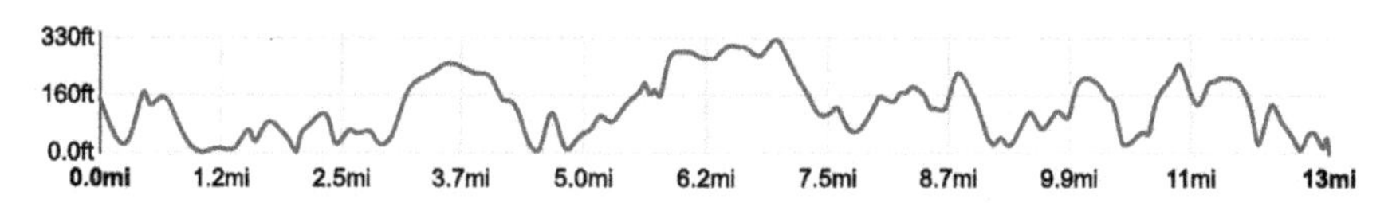

DIRECTIONS:

1. The coast path is picked up just by the right-hand side of the white entrance gates to Pentewan Sands. It is signed for the Coast Path. The path heads inland for a while and then the path splits. Take the left-hand path over the stile and now follow the path back to Mevagissey. Keep the sea on your left. If you find yourself on the footpath directly on the road, you have overshot the turning for the coast path.

2. As the path heads back towards the sea, there is an option to head down to a small cove called Portgiskey. It is also possible to access Portgiskey from Pentewan Sands, avoiding the hill path, but this is only possible at very low tide and may also involve some rock scrambling. **See *Portgiskey*.**

3. The path then continues to Meva and is quite arduous, with lots of ups and downs, although it is only about a mile. As the trail heads into Mevagissey, you will begin to pass some gardens to your right and a gate into Trevalsa Hotel on your right. Just after this, there is a path on your left down to Polstreath Beach. This is a lovely and often empty beach. Possibly because of the 100 steps.

4. Continuing along the coast path you start to look down on the harbour of Mevagissey, carry on down through the tiny lanes until you get onto the harbourside. **See *Harbour*.**

Portgiskey: There is a small collection of pilchard cellars. Pilchard fishing was the main industry of St Austell Bay. For reasons that are unclear the pilchard began to turn up in our waters in vast numbers. The whole of the St Austell Bay benefited from this bounty, but it was Mevagissey that was pre-eminent in the fishing industry. Although not particularly popular in Britain, the pilchard was highly sought after on the continent. At one point in the early 1900's, the St Austell Bay area exported around 75 million pilchards. To process the fish, they were first salted in brine tanks and then packaged in wooden casks. The casks had holes in the bottom, and a lid was placed on top to which weights were added in order to squeeze the oil from the fish. To further leverage the squeeze, a long pole was slotted into the hole in the wall, and weights were tied to the end of it. The pole rested on top of the lid and pressed the pilchard. The lids were then fitted, and the barrels were shipped out.

5. Start on Mevagissey's harbourside. From the harbour facing out to sea, walk to your right along the waterfront until you pass the tackle shop and just before the loos, take the steps up to Polkirt Hill. Walk uphill until you reach No.49, then take the footpath to your left. Continue to walk uphill. The pathway then splits, ahead to a large white building or right to re-join the road. For an excellent detour, walk towards the white flats and through the gate, take the path onto the Crow's Nest for great views of the harbour and beyond.

6. Return to the path and head up to the road. The coast path now continues uphill along the road. This can be busy and tight in summer; drivers can be very frustrated at this point so please walk with care. As the road levels out there is a road turning downhill to the left called Portmellon Road, take this road all the way down into Portmellon, around the cove and back up out of the village. As you start heading uphill, and out of the village, take Chapel Point Lane on your left. Continue along as it becomes a private drive and after you have passed three benches look out for a sign to your left for the coast path and take it. **See *Chapel Point.***

7. You are now on this path all the way to Gorran, traffic free. There will be some steps, stiles and sheep along the way as well as some steep cliffs. This section of the walk is about two miles. Dogs will need to be on a lead for many parts of it.

Harbour: The earliest evidence we have for the harbour is around 1550 when a stone quay was built in the general location of the existing East Quay, jutting out from the Harbour Masters office towards West Quay. West Quay is on the other side of the harbour and houses the Ice House and Fish Stores. The beach and slipway in front of where you are currently standing is known as Old Sand and is clearly where the fishing village began. The rocks behind, providing a level of protection that was then reinforced by the mediaeval harbour wall. This section of the harbour is known as Island Quay, and you can see in old paintings that these buildings were once accessed via a bridge.

Chapel Point: Few builders left such an enduring mark on the area as architect John Archibald Campbell. The three houses at the end of Chapel Point were designed by him. They are breath-taking examples of arts and craft architecture in the Scottish style. They were meant to be the forerunners of a Utopian housing project that he had successfully submitted plans for. Unfortunately one evening he walked off a cliff and died.

8. As you drop into Gorran, the coast path joins a residential lane, follow all the little lanes downhill until you get to the beach at Gorran Haven. This is your last refreshment stop for five miles.

9. From the beach, head towards the fish and chip shop and turn left onto Foxhole Lane, the coastpath is clearly marked ahead up a few steps. Follow the coastpath until you are looking down on a very large sandy beach. This is Vault Beach; it's a lovely beach but there is no way to rejoin the path at the other end of the beach. If you want to go down to the beach you can climb a path half way along the beach if you want. It is quite a slog up and down though. Continue along the coast path until you reach the Dodman. This a very demanding stretch of the coastpath as you climb up to the highest point of the South Cornish coast **See *Dodman Point*.**

10. Having stood at the Cross return to the coast path and walk along with the sea still on your left. Carry along the coast path until you see a footpath signed to Penare on your right. Just before this, there is a V shape stile that will take you up onto the very impressive cliff castle ramparts. WARNING. There are some very large rabbit holes along this ridge concealed by the overgrowth. Walk with care. The view up here is fabulous, and it is an incredible structure, to still be standing thousands of years later. At the end of this section, make your way back down to the path, this can be tricky and then take the path back to the coast path.

Dodman Point: Also known as Deadman's Point, this small headland holds a wealth of historical features

A huge granite cross was placed here in 1896 as a navigational aid to seafarers. Opposite the path to the cross, you can take a short diversion inland to the watch-house, a 1795 survivor of a series of Admiralty signal stations used to alert the Navy at Plymouth.

In the fields behind the cross, there are a whole range of archaeological features. These include a later prehistoric cliff castle, the very impressive Bulwarks, with two prehistoric round barrows, and a mediaeval field system, situated on Dodman Point, a prominent flat-topped headland projecting south into the English Channel, south-west of Gorran Haven. Also within the scheduled area are a mediaeval or later trackway and beacon, a Napoleonic signal station, a building, extraction pits, a field system, boundary stones and a cross of the 18th and 19th centuries, and two probable World War II bomb craters.

11. Continue along the coast path until you drop down onto Hemmick Beach. This is a small cove and popular with locals in summer, despite the adjacent road it is not easy to access, the road is very narrow and steep in both directions. Continue along the coast path It's about two miles to Porthluney beach at Caerhays. The path is mostly through fields and then down through a small wooded area. As you leave the woods you will see Caerhays Castle across the valley. Head down the fields and onto the road. This is a good place for refreshments; the café is highly rated.

12. The coast path now continues along the road, it's small but often busy. Keeping the sea on your left, walk along the road with the castle on your right. The road bends to the left and now climbs steeply. Walk up the hill and you pick up the coastpath again at the corner of the next bend in the road, this time to the right. Climb up the steps and through the kissing gate. Once through the gate turn right and follow the path with the hedge directly to your right This field and the next often contain cattle. There is also a scenic Coastwatch Station. **See *Caerhays Castle*.**

13. This is now a gentle section of the coastpath, mostly flat and even, and often awash with butterflies After a while it drops down into the twin fishing hamlets of East and West Portholland.

Caerhays Castle: The Castle was desiged in 1808 by the Georgian architect John Nash for the Williams family. J C Williams of Caerhays (1862 - 1939) gave up politics in 1895 and became passionate about gardening. He was quick to recognise the importance of the plant hunters' work and contributed £300,000 (in today's terms) of his own money towards Forrest's 1911 and subsequent expeditions, as well as being involved in the joint funding of many other trips.

COAST PATH SIGN

14. Depending on the state of the sea you can cross from East Portholland to West Portholland along the seawall, this is a bit of a scabble in places. If there are waves or a high tide, walk up the East Portholland road and keep an eye out for the coastpath sign on your left. Take this over to West Portholland. Once in West Portholland, whichever way you go, keep an eye out for the coastpath sign and head back up onto the path. The final two miles are very scenic, although the climb up out of Portholland is very steep. **See *Porhollands*.**

15. Halfway between Portholland and Portloe, there is a Bond Villain style house, just after you see this, the path suddenly becomes very steep and narrow and downhill. This section doesn't last long, but it is a little challenging especially on tired legs. As the walk comes to an end you walk down into the sheltered village of Portloe.

In return, Caerhays received a wealth of seed from newly discovered species of Chinese rhododendrons, magnolias, camellias, azaleas, acers and evergreen oaks to mention but a few. A large number of these unique plants can be seen growing in maturity at Caerhays today.

The arrival of this plant material opened up opportunities for JC and his successors, Charles and Julian Williams to engage in an extensive programme of hybridisation work which is still going on today. The origin of the truly hardy, free flowering and easy to grow x williamsii strain of camellias dates from J C's original cross between Camellia saluenensis and Camellia japonica in 1923. Williamsii hybrid camellias now number many thousands of varieties and are still hybridised and grown throughout the world.

The Porthollands: These two hamlets and the surrounding fields were base for the recent Hollywood blockbuster, Miss Peregrine's Home for Peculiar Children.

MEVAGISSEY

PHOTO ALBUM

https://www.flickr.com/photos/97473606@N04/sets/72157687363132270

GET INVOLVED!

Join Walkers Talk Back on Facebook, to read about the next book in the walking series. Suggest routes, give feedback, receive advance copies. Better yet, share photos and feedback of the walks you enjoyed.
https://www.facebook.com/groups/841952742623247/

Did you enjoy this book? You can make a big difference.

Reviews are very powerful and can help me build my audience. Independent authors have a much closer relationship with their readers, and we survive and thrive with your help.

If you've enjoyed this book, then you can leave a review on Goodreads.

If you read it online leave a review on the site where you purchased it

Thanks for helping.

HELLO AND THANK YOU

Getting to know my readers is really rewarding, I get to know more about you and enjoy your feedback, it only seems fair that you get something in return so if you sign up for my newsletter you get various free downloads, depending on what I am currently working on plus advance notice of new releases. I don't send out many newsletters, and I will never share your details. If this sounds good, click on the following: www.lizhurleyauthor.com

I'm also on all the regular social media platforms so look me up.

MORE BY LIZ HURLEY

A HISTORY OF MEVAGISSEY

An engaging and informative history of Mevagissey.

For over eight hundred years Mevagissey has flourished beside the south Cornish coastline. It has, in its heyday, been a globally significant port, lighting the streets of London in the eighteenth century and feeding the homes of Europe.

It has been battered by freak storms and a cholera outbreak but has continued, unbroken, contributing in no small part to the colonisation of the world by Cornish men and women.

This potted history gives an insight into the history of the village and takes a humorous look behind the scenes into what it is like to actually live and work in Cornwall's second largest fishing port. It debunks a few myths and introduces some lively, tall tales, as told through local voices.

Available in Bookshops.
Paperback: 9780993218026
Digital. Available on all platforms
https://www.books2read.com/mevagissey

SCRIBBLES FROM THE EDGE

When everyday life is anything but every day.

Liz Hurley gathers together her newspaper columns to deliver a collection of fast, funny reads. Join in as you share the highs and lows of a bookseller, dog lover and mother in Britain's finest county. This treasure trove of little gems moves from lifestyle pieces on living day-to-day, behind the scenes in the UK's number one tourist destination, to opinion pieces on education, current affairs, science, politics and even religion. Watching the sun set over a glowing beach isn't quite so much fun when you are trying to find the keys your child hid in the sand, and the tide is coming in! Join in and discover just how hard it is to surf and look glamorous at the same time. Batten down the hatches as she lets off steam about exploding cars and rude visitors. Laugh along and agree or disagree with Liz's opinion pieces, as you discover that although life might not be greener on the other side, it's a lot of fun finding out.

Available in Bookshops.
Paperback: 9780993218002
Digital. Available on all platforms
https://www.books2read.com/scribbles

LOSING IT IN CORNWALL

The second collection of columns from Liz Hurley, still scribbling away on the edge. Still trying to hold it together. From serious to silly her columns cover all that life throws at us. A perfect selection of little titbits, to pick up and put down or read straight through.

Available in Bookshops.
Paperback: 9780993218019
Digital. Available on all platforms
https://www.books2read.com/losing-it

Lightning Source UK Ltd.
Milton Keynes UK
UKHW020648070619
344040UK00009B/150/P